ANN Bridge DAVIES is an accredited working medium and spirit artist who has drawn spirit portraits and given verbal evidence, about the spirit people she sees clairvoyantly, to thousands in many countries of the world for over thirty years. She creates the spirit portraits because she wants to help people understand that although the physical body dies, and returns to the earth, our integral spirit, the part of us which is our core persona, remains alive and can be recreated as works of art. A drawing of a man, woman, child or animal, who Ann has never met, is drawn in seconds to the surprise of all watching and can give hope to both those who watch and those who receive the beautiful portraits of their family members or friends who they thought they would never see again.

This book is simply about an ordinary girl who draws the people she sees and, later, as an adult, realises the drawings can be passed on to their loved ones. She is currently researching the History of Spirit Art for her postgraduate degree and has presented papers on spirit and psychic art for the British Psychological Society-Transpersonal Section and Exploring the Extraordinary Conference at York University as well as lecturing and teaching spirit art.

*

PORTRAITS FROM SPIRIT

ANN BRIDGE DAVIES

www.anndavies-artofspirit.co.uk

AuthorHouse™ UK Ltd.
500 Avebury Boulevard
Central Milton Keynes, MK9 2BE
www.authorhouse.co.uk
Phone: 08001974150

First published by AuthorHouse 5/24/2011

ISBN: 978-1-4567-7497-4 (sc)

Acknowledgements

Thank you
to the many friends and family members who have had to put up with me for
the past year whilst finishing this book.
Special thanks to Rod, Becky, Eric, Paul, Dorothy, June, Alan, Janet, Shirley
and Mellissa for help and support along the journey.

*

Namaste
*

This book:

PORTRAITS FROM SPIRIT

Is dedicated to all past, present and future
Spirit and Psychic Artists

*

CONTENTS

Introduction

Is it possible that we, as human beings, are capable of communicating from the grave to our friends and loved ones who we have left behind in the mortal earth world? Is it also possible that deceased artists are able to utilise the abilities they had before death in order to draw portraits of those who have also died, through the hand of a living artist? Yes, I believe all the above to be true. Not only do I believe the statement above to be true I also *know* the statement to be true since I have spent a large part of my life drawing and painting thousands of proven portraits from the supposedly invisible world of the dead, in order to help others understand that when we die we do not completely disappear.

This book is about my life, work and passion as a spirit artist, lecturer and exhibitor, demonstrating how I have been able to draw and paint the world of the afterlife, and how I now feel the need to pass on the detail, process and methodology underpinning these, paranormally motivated, unusual art techniques surrounding spirit art, to those who want to know and experience the phenomenon for themselves. As far back as I can remember I have had the abilities of an artist and clairvoyant medium but it was through my ability as an artist that I felt the compulsion to create images of the things I could see, hear and sense from the invisible, to some, world of spirit. The impressions I saw were of spirit faces, landscapes and objects illuminated with beautiful pearlescent light. I recreated the spirit impressions as drawings and paintings so that others could also see the images I experienced and sensed paranormally.

As early as four I remember that I was capable of creating artworks, in pastel, paint, charcoal or any other mark making material I had in my art box, which did not seem to be of this world. My artwork appeared to communicate messages, both visual and verbal, to those who could not 'see' their family or friends' post-mortem, as I could, and who struggled to understand the concept of life after death. I felt the need to help them see what I could see and, through the process of art, I was able to do just that, I was able to paint portraits they could recognise and cherish.

One of the first portraits I remember creating was a profile portrait of a young African woman whose hair was beaded tight to her head with neck rings coiling around the ebony toned skin. The image, which stirred my art teacher at school to give me an 'A' for effort and attainment, was not inspired from something seen on TV or in a book but by a spirit model quietly sitting for her portrait to be drawn by me. Of course, as a child, I could never tell anyone where my inspiration came from. To inquirers it was always 'made up out of my head' not part of the invisible world of the afterlife. As a child these impressions and thoughts remained very close to my heart because I did not want to upset anyone. However, as I grew older, the 'cat jumped out of the bag' and, although not understanding what I was doing completely, also knowing my family wouldn't relish the idea of their daughter or sister talking to dead people, I spoke little of it.

This book explains how, in my childhood, I thought that those I saw in the spirit world could be seen by everybody. I was under that impression because my family never spoke of such matters and I reasoned that I could see these, invisible to most, wonderful spirit people more clearly because I was an artist. How wrong and naïve I was. It was much later in life that I found this not to be true and, as an artist, and later a spiritualist medium, I was, over the years, able to put my 'visions' to good use. The process of drawing and painting the world of spirit came easy to me and many of the scenes depicted in my paintings had come from that world. However, the idea of being a medium between two worlds, although as natural to me as breathing, and having been born with the ability to see, hear and sense the spirit of those who had died, needed to be developed. It was not until I was in my mid thirties that I was able to publicly demonstrate what is now known as psychic or spirit portraiture. From that point I have never looked back. I have now retired from my day-to-day employment as a Head of Art in secondary education, art lecturer and assessor, and am now only working with the images and impressions I receive from another world, vibration, dimension, existence, call it what you want. To me the spirit world is a place of light and great love and is a place, I believe, we all return to after death.

As a teacher I can't let a book I have written go out of my hands without some sort of guidance for prospective spirit artists. I have included information detailing the content of workshops and courses I have taught around the world. This includes the lessons I have learnt in teaching the courses and workshops, as well as information I have gained from my students. This information I can pass on to the reader, and potential spirit artist, as guidance to those of you who have an interest in art and think may also have mediumistic tendencies. I have written in such a way that you will be able to see if some of the supernatural experiences in your life are similar to mine, or that of my students and, perhaps, this will help you to decide to join those spiritualist mediums who give comfort and light to those who are seeking their loved ones in spirit. But also, to give you help in choosing whether to take the chance to put those people, places and objects you have been seeing, super-normally, onto paper, for everyone to see.

I write about how I developed my skills and how you, the reader, can develop the basis of spirit art yourself. I give examples of my own experiences together with those of my students and the people who have received the portraits when I have demonstrated spirit art in public. I hope this book may help you to understand that, although mediumship is very rewarding, it can also be a difficult path to tread, and life often does not seem easier but often more uphill and rocky. But, what I say is; "It is the end product together with the people you meet and the experiences you encounter on the journey which matter the most!"

I wish a safe journey to those who embark upon the spiritual path towards creating, guiding and helping others through the archway towards spirit art.

Chapter One

BURTON BRADSTOCK AND THE BEWILDERING MIDSUMMER FAYRE

The old Dorset village hall was bathed in sunlight as my friend Rosie and I walked up to the ancient scratched and kicked-in front door. Restless dogs, children and adults were queuing to get into the summer Fayre. It was 1978 and I was on holiday with an old college friend caravanning in the quaint English village of Burton Bradstock. My friend was aware that the village always put on a good selection of homemade jams, cakes and locally grown vegetables just for a few pence to get in, because this had been her favourite holiday haunt since she was a child.

It was August during the school summer holidays and hotter than usual that day. We were thirsty for the expected goodies beyond and, when we finally entered the hall through the old wooden doors, the evocative sweet smell of home cooked produce hit us together with a solid stream of people entering the hall. Just as we were surrounded by the hustle and bustle of milling people the sun, full strength at mid-day, blazing through an un-curtained window, hit my eyes, blinding me for a few moments, until all became clear again. As I stood for a while, my senses soaking up the atmosphere, my friend, interested in the pickles and veggies for dinner, sped off towards a crowded stall, I noticed a queue forming by the be-curtained village stage with a home-made sign saying; 'Have your palm read today... only a pound'! 'Well why not' I thought, 'I've never had it done before and it can't do any harm'.

I joined the queue with nervous anticipation not realising there would be about a forty minute wait in the hot stuffy hall. Rosie joined me, taking the same view that the palm reading would be a bit of fun. Never having come across anything like this before I was unsure of what to expect. At the time I was aware I saw unusual things but was not aware that it was the supernatural world and so did not categorise what was to happen as a serious paranormal event.

Eventually the stage side curtains opened and I was asked to climb onto the platform, through the velvet drapes and into a small room beyond. I turned to Rosie who smiled back and said, "Don't be too long, I've got an ice cream waiting for me." I could smell the dust from back-stage as I spread the curtains and walked onto the wooden boards. A slit of light from the door jamb of the side room was beckoning and, unusually for me, I began to feel nervous. The door creaked as I pushed it open. I entered a half lit room with dim light cascading through some ancient net curtains. A woman in black Victorian clothing was sitting behind a small table asking me to move forward and sit on an old wooden school chair. Her head was covered by a black veil and as she moved her hand towards mine I noticed the age spots and wrinkles on her hand...she was very old.

"I can see from your hand that art will rule your life."

This first comment threw me, how did she know I was an artist? I was visiting dressed just like any other person on holiday in shorts and tee-shirt, how could she see that? "You will show others what you know to the end of your life. You will teach not only art but other subjects which are more esoteric, psychic and spiritual." Another shock to my mind; how did she know I was a teacher? The reading continued as she spoke about emotional relationships, where I would live and the work I would do, most of which I can't remember now. After about twenty minutes she let go of my hand, now very warm and clammy, and asked me to pay the person by the curtain. I was overwhelmed, the questions going through my mind were to do with mind reading, how could she know all these things, did she know someone I knew, how did she know what I did for a living?

Finding my way off the stage in the semi darkness I paid the elderly lady sitting like a guard, half in and half out of the stage curtain, allowing nobody to leave without paying. Rosie was waiting and enquired as to how the reading went before she took her chance with the unknown. I was so shocked I couldn't speak. I suggested we discussed our readings when she came out. Very hot and confused I went to get an ice cream. The sun was hot and at its highest, but just being outside was a welcome relief. Sitting on a low stone wall, ice cream in hand, I pondered my apparent fate. How did she know just by looking at my hand I was an artist and art teacher? Where did she find the clues to my future life and destiny and what was all this psychic stuff about?

Rosie joined me a little while later to say that she was also fascinated by the reading she had just been given but she didn't say much about the detail so I left it at that. As college friends we both came from families where mediumship and the paranormal were never discussed. That was our first experience of the mystical world of the supernatural, or so I thought. I had not considered the apparitions I saw as a child to be in the same league as to what had just happened. I had seen and spoken with the spirit world since I was a child, yet, in my innocence of such matters, I thought that I saw those visions and happenings because I was an artist and I also thought that *all* artists saw another world invisible to many. Although intrigued by the experience in Burton Bradstock, after the holiday I thought nothing of it. I did not make the connection between the spirit world I had experienced as a child and the message from the palmist-medium at that time, like waiting for a train; I had to wait for the connection to be made.

My spirit was born into the body of Ann Jacqueline Bridge, third in a family of four children and the only girl. I arrived on the earth in the month of April, 1950, in Knotty Ash, Liverpool, England, at 9.20pm, an hour before my twin brother, who was not expected! Together with my brothers I had a Roman Catholic upbringing where, for a child, the philosophy of the religion was difficult to understand, because this was at a time when the Catholic mass was said in Latin. However, without realising it at the time, the mystical concepts of that religion were, and have remained, firmly embedded within my psyche.

The 1950's were also a time when children were seen and not heard. Children did not have a voice in the family, they were told what to do and they did it or were chastised by the parents, and sometimes the priest. There was no television to watch but I do remember the Queen's coronation with everyone huddled around a neighbour's black and white TV in 1953. 'Catch a Falling Star' is one of the popular songs I remember gently emanating from the family radio in the living room while I watched the snow silently fall in the winter of 1956, when most of Britain was contained under three to twelve feet of snow. This was a family, and perhaps also a time, when theories of the afterlife were discussed only between adults or never spoken about at all.

I had my 'invisible' friend who I chatted to when I was alone in my own bedroom for fear of ridicule from my elder brother, whose sarcasm could be equally as humorous as hurting for a young girl. My 'friend' would chat at night and my parents would hear me 'talking to myself' from the time I could speak. Laughing and chatting in a childish gobble-de-gook, which amused my parents, I would spend time each night developing a connection with the invisible world only I knew about.

In August 1958 my family moved from the Knotty Ash house, now too small for three growing boys, to the house which belonged to my mother's side of the family in Stoneycroft, Liverpool 13. I was eight and the paranormal experiences, although already evident in the waking and lucid dreaming states of my mind, appeared mainly when half asleep when there would be episodes of watching apparitions in a very beautiful place. There was nothing to really speak about regarding the spirit people until we moved to the new house, the relocation seeming to exacerbate the sightings and occurrences of more spirit people unknown to me, although, strangely enough, in a world which never frightened but intrigued me.

'Dentdale' was built in 1864 for my great-grandfather, Reverend Christopher Anthony Carter, long since departed this world for the next, and subsequently owned by his spinster daughters, Lily and Daisy Carter. The day I met the sisters for the first time they were dressed as though they had come straight out of a Victorian magazine. Their hair was long, but plaited and coiled up tightly at the back of their heads, white lace at the neck and cuffs under black satin jackets and skirts. Two very pleasant ladies who on reflection, were representations of the 'Girls Own' Christmas edition books, dated 1901, from the library in the front morning room of the house. The sisters served us cucumber sandwiches on thin white crustless bread before we were shown around what was, to those who had come from a small house, a huge five bed-roomed property. They were both artists in their own right and many of their large landscape oil paintings were still hanging on the walls until my mother's move from the house at the age of 96.

Reverend CA Carter and Family
photographed around 1905 in the garden at Tynwald Hill, Liverpool

As Ann Jacqueline Bridge my birth was the beginning of a mortal life with the twists and turns everybody has to go through. To grow up, to fall in love, to be hurt emotionally and physically, to bear children, to grow old, to be told I have been born with the disease Genetic Haemochromatosis

7

at the age of 55 and will have to undergo life-long hospital treatment in a hospital cancer ward, all these events merely aspects of which a human life goes through, unless we are tremendously lucky. However, it was at this time as a child, I realised that I was not just a physical being with the genetic inheritances from my parents and ancestors; I also had a *spirit* which was different from, but immersed within, my physical body. This mind blowing theory came to me together with an experience I will never forget as I slept in the room in the house in which my great-grandfather died (my mother had informed me of this when we moved into the house), in fact she also said that most of her family had died there. The history of the room did not concern me, however in the years to come there were many supernatural occurrences which happened predominately in that room where I slept.

The experience that initiated the idea that we exist before and after our earth life occurred one morning as I woke, yet was unable to move my physical body. I lay motionless, in the warmth of the bed, paralysed from head to foot. I remember the moment and the thoughts clearly in my head. I was comfortable but unable to raise my fingers or toes, or any part of my body, and yet, I was still able to have thoughts! 'I can't move my head, my legs, my hands, any part of my body, but I can still think! How is it possible that I am I able to think when I can't move? Is this like being dead?' My mind was racing. 'Are my thoughts [my mind] different from my body, in a different place [existence]?' I was only ten engaging in esoteric thoughts more likely to come from a philosopher than a child.

This was the beginning of a life packed full of supernatural, paranormal and sometimes unbelievable experiences that were not openly discussed in my family and I had to wait until late in my adulthood, when the connections to people, places and experience, came along and I felt the time was right. The following pages tell the story of the people, places and events I have experienced while passing in and out of the world of spirit. As an artist and medium between the two worlds I have been able to draw, describe and paint what I can see in the afterlife. Experiencing **is** believing and I hope that I can pass on, through the words in this book, the visualisations, manifestations and supernatural happenings for you, the reader, to experience too.

I have been able to understand the difference between my etheric or spirit body since the experience I had at the age of ten because my adult belief has been rooted in those experiences. An inner knowing that each living being on the earth has been born with a duality of existence which is commonly known in psychic circles as the *physical* body and the *spirit* body and that in life these two bodies are amalgamated. One body being solid, the other etheric and invisible, both housed within the one being and both *alive*. I came to this conclusion after having the profound spiritual experience as a child, by not being able to move my body, and with my mind still working clearly, my belief has been formed that we all have a spirit that's invisible to many yet is able to work together with, and also independently from, our physical body, whilst living and breathing on this planet called Earth.

As a child I slept in the small front room in a bed with a feather mattress. On those freezing wintry nights when the ice formed as 'snow-leaves' on the inside of the Victorian sash window, the snug sensation of the feathers moulding around my body, was a delight to the senses. Before flopping into the double size mattress, leaving the arctic temperatures of the bedroom behind, I would be fully dressed in a fleecy nightdress, plus dressing gown and woolly socks, to keep out the cold. At a time in history when children did not have a TV, iPods' or computers in their bedrooms at night, I would, after turning out the light, open the curtains so I could watch and make imaginary pictures out of the tops of the poplar trees dancing in the wind of the night. Sometimes when the sky was clear enough for the moon, with its brilliant silvery light flowing into the room, I would watch the translucent arc it made across the sky, thinking deeply about aspects of life beyond my childhood reasoning.

At this young age, when these existentialist thoughts started to form in my mind, I watched the clouds, trees, stars, sun and moon dictate the theatrical visual effects I would see with my young innocent eyes, it was then that I had my first real understanding of the difference between the body and the mind. At that that time I began to see and speak to people who would come to visit me both at night and in the day, especially the 'Boy' who would stand and talk to my mother while she was cooking or washing up in the kitchen. At first I would talk to my parents and siblings about these people but I was always shouted down and told I was imagining things, like a child imagines a gown on the back of the bedroom door as a gorilla after the bedroom light has been turned out. However, my persistence regarding the Boy who followed my mother around the kitchen was not paid-off kindly. As I described the young man to her as being about 18 years old with sticky-out ears and bushy brown hair and a cheeky smile with a fish in his hand (he was someone I was not afraid of because he seemed a nice person and seemed to know my mother) I was taken straight to the priest to be talked to about lying!

My mother had recognised the young man as her brother who died in a tragic accident in Thornborough, Yorkshire, while catching fish for the cats in a water wheel while it was switched off in his lunch hour from work. Apparently, while he was inside the wheel someone switched it on and he was killed. The shock was so great to my mother and her family, he was never spoken about, it all seemed too painful for them and so when I began talking about him and laughing when he showed me funny tricks, it caused problems. I was instantly taken to see Father Cottrell, a tall elderly, Irish sounding man, for extra Catechism! He did not believe I was seeing the dead, and anyway I was not allowed to, he said it was forbidden. So while my brothers were enjoying 'Sinbad the Sailor' at the children's matinee in the cinema just around the corner from the church, I was sitting in a sparse, smelly priest's house with an elderly man preaching at me. The only good those sessions did for me was to keep me quiet. Later on, when I saw people in my mind's eye or externally, like solid people, those people no-one else could see, I would just keep quiet about it. And so I did, until I realised that I had a specific talent which I should work with and develop.

Yes, when the body dies the mind, which 'thinks' in life, still continues and it is that mind, from a physically deceased person, which communicates with me, as a medium, from another dimension of existence. After my childhood experiences the sightings of the spirit people started to diminish in the house and some of them were never seen again. I am sure they got their message across to me and although they may still have been present in the house I stopped seeing them. They never frightened me because I had realised that they all belonged to my mother's family and although most of the spirit people were old in looks they were not scary. I never thought of them as ghosts I suppose, because I felt I knew them, they were still family.

Childhood and growing up took over. I returned to visiting the thrilling matinee cinema on a Saturday morning, playing in the local park at weekends and holidays and spending time drawing and painting when the weather was inclement. During my teenage years I did well at secondary school, going from not passing my 11 plus exam to passing all my GCE's and CSE's, and the only pupil from my Secondary School moving up to the Grammar School to do A-levels. The Beatles, Cliff Richard and Elvis Presley were top of my agenda with Mum taking me to some concerts because she was part of the Red Cross First- Aid contingency at their concerts. I was also lucky enough to see Bob Dylan in 1966 at the Liverpool Empire; the thought of ghosts and spirit people was as far away from my mind as the North Pole. Pop groups, boys, art and drama were my thing as a follower of fashion during the 60's belonging to the Liverpool Youth Theatre and the Everyman Youth Theatre at that exciting time in Liverpool.

However it was in August 1971 when I had an experience which at the time I was not aware was connected to the Devonshire palmist incident, but as I look back on my life, I realise there were several moments in time which have led to me writing this book today. Again it was in the hot summertime when the incident occurred.

I had returned from Matlock College of Education after being awarded my Certificate in Education, having gained two distinctions in Art Practice and Teaching. I was one out of four hundred students who was asked back to College to take the Bachelor of Education degree in Art teaching, which was a new degree at the time. It meant another year at college but it gave me a degree which I had never thought I could achieve at the time. As part of the CertEd I loved learning about educational psychology and took the opportunity to study psychology as part of the B.Ed. degree with art. It meant an extra year with Nottingham University education department and I knew it would put a stretch on my parents' income but I had learnt to live on nothing and knew I could do that again for a short while. What happened that summer, before I began my academic future, took over fifteen years to recover from emotionally, and, from which, my mother never recovered. If I had known then what I know now about death and dying I may not have made so many blunders in my life to come.

My first profoundly paranormal experience of any significance was in the spring of 1971. Not only were the Beatles all the rage in Liverpool, I was about to see my first solid spirit ghost. It was June and I had just returned from College with my teaching certificate. I felt good and happy with the way my life was going. I was asleep with my head under the bed covers shielding me from a slight chill in the air. Around 3.00am there was a distinct change in the atmosphere in the bedroom and I became aware of a light in the centre of the room. My bed was against the interior wall side-on to a large sash window but it seemed too early for the sun to be rising and wondered what was causing light? As I moved the sheet from my face I began to see the light at the bottom of my bed getting brighter and brighter and within a few seconds the solid form of a small round-bodied nun in full black and white habit emerged. In my half sleep state I was confused at the reason why there was a nun in my bedroom and started to panic. The nun smiled and as though she was thinking her thoughts to me I heard these words distinctly in my head, "everything will all be alright - you may not think so at the time but please believe me it will". I gasped and quickly covered my face with the sheets only to lower them again after an undetermined length of time. There was no longer any sign of her - she had disappeared! I had a feeling she was talking about my father but was not sure.

I was unable to comprehend what had happened to me or why, I was speechless, this image remains as clear today as it was those many years ago. Why was a nun in my bedroom in the middle of the night and speaking with her mind, without opening her mouth? What was the meaning of it all? That summer was full of surprises and the reason for the appearance of the angelic nun became clear approximately four months later after a life changing event at home in Liverpool. The manifestation of the spirit nun played on my mind all summer but I said nothing of the event to my parents, family or friends, for fear of ridicule and misunderstanding. I had no idea who she was and have never felt the need to find out, but her words repeated in my mind like a stuck record going over and over again until her words were prophetically fulfilled.

It was August, one of those sultry English summer days when the temperature is hot but the sky overcast and one of those days when you wouldn't know what to wear in case of rain. My brothers were out somewhere and my father had a little time off from work to fix some floorboards in the old worn-out house. I could hear the banging of the hammer on the boards as he set the nails home. He was very clever at fixing anything broken; from wall sockets to slates on the roof. He could set his hand to anything, and he did. There was a smell of kerosene filling the house with which he was painting the damaged boards. It is a smell which always takes me back to those fated moments in the family home.

This was the day when the nun's words suddenly became clear. This was the day my father ceased to exist as part of the material world when he died of a blockage to the heart and could not have survived even with expert help. It is not his untimely passing which is important to the essence of this book; it is what occurred several weeks after she spoke to me which gave me an insight confirming the nun's words were not in vain.

On that August afternoon I had been making a cup of tea in the kitchen when my father, grey in the face, clutching at the shirt on his chest, asked me to phone the doctor. Not knowing where the phone book was I tried to find the number but was unable to do so. He asked me to call out for my uncle (who was visiting England from Belgium) but he was soaking in the bath and my father and I both knew there was little time for him to get dressed. My father said he was going to drive to the hospital where my mother was working as a nurse. We climbed into the car and I sat in the passenger seat with him while he drove. He was in so much pain I had to hold the steering wheel for him while he went through the several red lights on the way. I was a non-driver at the time and found the experience terrifying, not knowing if my father was going to make it to the hospital in time. Later we were told that it was a miracle he managed to reach where he wanted to go. We went straight to the emergency ward which was empty and no-one to help. I knew the ward my mother was working on and ran with the speed of a jaguar to get to her. When I arrived I could hear the sound of a doctor's emergency bleeper telling the Doctor to go to the emergency ward where my father was alone. I found Mum and we rushed back to the room where he was laying on a hospital bed. I could hear that his breathing was laboured and I wanted to help but was ushered away by a nurse into a visitor's room. My mother stayed with the doctor to help but my feeling was that it was no good. He had managed to get to, and be with, the one he loved while fighting for his life.

I could not tell you how many minutes it was before my mother, as white as a sheet, came to the visitor's room door to tell me that my father had died and she was staying in the ward to be with him. I left the hospital and got a bus to a friend's house only to find he wasn't home. At a time when mobile phones were not in existence and public phones were few and far between I was not able to contact him before I arrived at his house. He wasn't home, so, sitting alone on the doorstep, I was given time to adjust to the shock of what had just happened. I stayed for a while and then, as the sun was going down in the clear blue sky, I left to return home as dusk fell.

It was a while later, after the shock had subsided, that I realised that this was why the nun had visited me seemingly to warn me of his passing. I have always thought of the supernatural meeting as being a forewarning of the imminent passing of my father. Her words of explanation that, 'all would be alright', encouraged me to understand that this was the moment my father was meant to return home to spirit and when I think about it now, I am sure I was meant to have that profound experience so that I would be able to understand the process of death and dying in order to help others. Helping me understand my own mediumship has been a crucial part of my paranormal development which has been strengthened more and more since that time.

Billy Bridge's funeral was arranged for the 23rd August 1971 a few weeks before I was due to return to University in late September. However, there was still one more event which was to create a bridge between the death of my father and my belief and understanding of life existing after death. My views based on there being a life after death were solidified after an occurrence, witnessed by myself and several people, a few weeks after my father's funeral. It is commonly thought that a funeral is the time the spirit of the deceased person is most in evidence, and a time for the spirit of the deceased to say goodbye to their loved ones and 'be at rest', but, in my father's case the full passage into spirit occurred much later. There was nothing spooky, nothing seems extreme to me now, just an extraordinary event where my father's spirit manifested in our house, at a time when *he* was ready to do so and could 'move on'.

The experience I had was jointly witnessed by three very sane people and was undoubtedly orchestrated by the spirit of my father. The day was overcast with little wind. There was a chill in the air inside the stone built house. My mother and two of my father's closest friends were in the house, having not seen us since the day of the funeral, and they were helping my grief stricken mother by making sandwiches in the small scullery kitchen. It was nothing special just sandwiches made from the bits and pieces Mum had in the larder.

The four of us had sat down at the living room table to eat our lunch. My mother and her friends were deep in thought, my mother justifiably still wearing her 'widow's weeds' when we heard the heavy front door open and close. The keys, always left in the vestibule door, jingled as the door was opened, and the sound of footsteps was heard to move from the door up the stairs. The air was chilled but very still around us as we looked at each other in puzzlement. We wondered which other members of the family had come home for lunch. We heard the sound of someone slowly climbing the stairs; the sound was like my father's, unique–to-him, footfall with the clink of the unbuckled sandals he used to wear. Not thinking of any other reason I mentioned to our friends that there may be another for lunch and suggested that my twin brother had arrived home.

Opening the living room door, I shouted up the stairs to ask my twin if he would like some lunch. No reply. I shouted again this time more insistently knowing I had a typical school-teacher's voice which could be heard above most things. There was still no reply. Irritated, I walked upstairs to ask him again. He was not in his bedroom, he was not in the bathroom, and, in fact, he was not in the house, he had not returned home at all!

An unpleasant sensation surrounded me and the hair rose on the back of my head. What on earth had we just witnessed? We definitely heard the door open and the sound of someone walking up the stairs, but who was it? I hurried back down the stairs to speak to our visitors. By then my mother had finished her lunch and was making a drink of tea and, so as not to alarm her, I spoke to my parents' friends who were just as confused as I was about the visiting footsteps. It sounded like my father's footsteps, the steps I had heard most of my life climbing the well trodden Victorian semi-carpeted stairs. We all agreed that the sound was very like my father and someone

15

squeezed directly behind it and, as they moved, I shuffled to the back of a very hot crowded room. The lady giving the talk pointed to me and said; "we have been waiting for you – you are the lady in red." Everybody turned around to look at me and nodded. "The very first spirit drawing I did was not taken by anyone and I was told it was for the 'lady in red', and here you are, and this is your drawing." She looked vaguely familiar to me as she spoke about the drawing and it was handed to me through the crowd. It was a black and white spirit-guide drawing of an Aztec woman which made absolutely no sense to me at the time. As the meeting ended and the crowd melted away, I made my way to the lady and realised she was my student teacher from ten or so years before, Miss Nichols. That night Linda had opened my mind to other modes of belief in saying that there was no such thing as coincidence. "Life just is!"

In writing this book, and revisiting the time I have just written about above, I am reminded that coincidences are just one of the examples of how the spirit world can take us to situations which will be important in our future life, and, maybe, change our life altogether. Miss Nichols the spirit artist did not know I would be attending that meeting, indeed I did not know until late in the evening that I was actually going to be there. Billy said later that he knew the call from abroad would not happen and that I would be there at the meeting. He had not spoken to the artist about our conversation in the street and so the drawing was a message to tell me I was in the right place at the right time and to open up to the possibility that there may be spirit people helping me from the 'other side'. When I left the gathering that night I was still puzzled over how and why I received that drawing and my confusion made matters worse when, at the next meeting I went to, I missed a message from my father altogether!

A few weeks had passed by and I decided to go to another of Billy's evenings. This time I was at the meeting place early but I still had to sit on the floor by the windows because the room again was crowded. The medium was introduced as Eddie Grenyer from Runcorn, a smartly dressed man in his late thirties standing to the front of the audience. I could just see him between the backs of the chairs in front of me. He spoke a little about the spirit world and what he was going to do that evening. I didn't really understand then the process and techniques mediums would use but was fascinated by the theatre of it all. For his first link he spoke a message from, what he called the spirit world. He said the name Jacqueline, a connection with twins, a birthday in April, the name Billy who passed to spirit with a condition of the heart and an Uncle Frank. He spoke carefully and compassionately but no one spoke up so he said he felt the person was confused and he would go onto the next link.

Again my heart was pounding…why did he give **my** name, Jacqueline, the name which only my family use, he gave out the month of **my** birthday, the fact that I am a twin, **my** father's name was Billy who passed with a heart condition and my favourite uncle who took his own life was called Frank? I was confused about the whole thing! I spoke to Eddy later and asked him why he gave all that information. He explained quite simply that in the spirit world, those who have died and who may be family members or friends, wanted to talk to me through him as the medium, between the physical earth world and the spirit world, and I had missed the chance. Eddy said it was like being the telephone line between the two worlds and those in spirit only have a short time to call. He said that he thought I should sit in circle with Billy to learn more, which I did. He did not say I was a medium or a spirit artist, that information came later.

On being invited to, and taking part at, Billy's home circle I found that I was able to see clairvoyantly and I could have trained as a psychic reader but involving myself with an invisible world of the 'dead' was frowned upon and, as a catholic school teacher, even more-so. When I mentioned I was sitting in a séance and going to the Spiritualist Church, Ken Lesser, a wonderful cartoonist, very humorous man and the third teacher in my art department at school, warned me off working with the dead. He was a Freemason and said that in his experience, some 'evil' things could happen to me if I didn't mark his words. I often wondered what he meant by that statement because I never really understood what his idea of evil was, since the concept has never really been part of my life. I understand that people act in a certain way because that is the way their physical brain and emotions work. The way I see it is that when we die we do not have a physical brain, and, if I understand the workings of the brain correctly, the brain, together with the nurturing, education and other experiences in life, good and bad, makes us who we are in the physical body. Without the physical body any 'evil' personality traits should disappear as we become our discarnate spirit. This is a very important area in the understanding of what actually happens to us after death so I will leave this open to debate at the moment, however, in my spiritual work I have never experienced the evil which Ken thought I would in my work as a medium so it is not easy for me to factually discuss. A very good book to read about the subject is *Life beyond Death* (2009) by David Fontana (d.2010).

However, I continued my psychic and spiritual development knowing that if my father was looking after me then nothing should go wrong. I joined Daulby Street Spiritualist Church in Liverpool and, under the guidance of trance medium Glyn Edwards, I developed my spiritual knowledge and understanding of the world of spirit and how we, in the mortal body, fit into the scheme of life. When we look back on our lives, certain occurrences in life seem to have been orchestrated by the spirit world. The meeting my husband was directed in many ways by the unseen world because In 1989 I was married by the now Spiritualist Officient Mr Edwards at Daulby Street Church, Liverpool, and shortly afterwards moved to the Midlands. The meeting and marriage was foretold by messages from several mediums, ranging from, "By the time I am 40 I will be married with two children" (I was married at 39 years of age and lost one child but also gave birth to one ten days before I was 40). On May 27th 1988 Tommy Richardson gave the name of my future husband together with what he did for work and said, "You will meet him before the end of May", and, astonishingly, I did!

My daughter, born in 1990, was given her spirit name the same year in Wolverhampton Spiritualist Church by Tony Gleeson, and nineteen years later I received, from the Spiritualist National Union, my certificates in demonstrating spiritualist mediumship (CSNUd) and public speaking on the philosophy of mediumship and spiritualism, (CSNUp). In order to achieve the certificates I had to go through rigorous assessment but they provide a certain amount of proof that I have the ability to be able to communicate with the spirit world. It had taken almost five decades to understand and recognise that even though we, as human beings, have a physical thinking existence on the planet earth, we also have an invisible spirit mind which 'lives' within us every day we are in existence in the physical world, and plays an important part in the lives of each and every one of us. We are all 'mediums' to the spirit world to some degree, let us cherish that fact and understand exactly how and why it works.

When looking back on our lives we can see patterns emerge which do not seem of our making. I wonder, if I had not taken the opportunity to go on holiday to Dorset with Rosie would I have developed as a medium and spirit artist. Did the palm reader place just enough future information into my psyche to enable me to bridge the gap between my artistry and mediumship or would the whole episode have happened anyway? My father would still have died and I would still have met Linda and Billy because those events were not mentioned in the reading. Looking at the patterns of my life I can see many different events which would have brought me to the same end, especially some of the events which inspired my involvement with, and, exploration of, spiritualism, mediumship and the writing of this book.

Chapter Two

GHOSTLY ANCESTORS INHABITING OUR HOUSE

The memories I have of the family home are always about being alone in an old, musty, rambling, house which was cold in the winter and warm in the summer. It may seem strange that even having quite a large family there was still a sense of loneliness and melancholy in the house and I wonder now, as an adult and am looking back over the long-gone-by days, why I only remember the certain events and the most vivid aspects of my life as a child and young adult? Is it because I was a very sensitive child in a place where there was little understanding of all the paranormal things I could see, hear, sense and smell in that old house? I never felt it was my home, it was always known as 'the house', because I was gradually becoming aware that my home may not be in this physical dimension at all but where those people, who came and went from my sight in the flicker of an eye, came from. The place I now know as being the *spirit world*.

Arriving at the Carter family house in the summer of 1958 was like going back to Victorian days, untouched for many a decade. The bell for the servants was still above the living room door, the front morning- room was as it had been since the time of my grandfather where he would write his sermons in the 1870's onwards. The back room, fitted with an upright piano, red velvet covered chaise-longue and an open fire place, had French windows facing out into the large garden where the two ladies would sit and read. The four bedrooms and two roomed attic which were furnished with feather mattress beds and large Victorian solid-wood bedroom furniture still remained in place until the house was closed after my mother left in 2010. This house was a mansion in comparison with the 'three bed semi' in Knotty Ash where we came from! The Carter family house, like something out of a Charles Dickens novel, offered an added dimension to those who could 'see' (and were sensitive) to the other world' that of ghosts!

As a child I would sit for hours in the front room; drawing, painting and completing my homework, away from the TV and teenage bickering from my brothers who would always be in the living room often waiting for their meal to be served if they hadn't already made the meal for themselves. I would also sit with my wheelchair-confined Irish Grandmother, when she stayed with us, chatting to her about experiences at school, the drawings I may be doing at the time or even sharing the recent ghost-stories I had heard. It was never said but I think I must have frightened my paternal Grandmother because she didn't stay very often. The ghosts I refer to were those who were part of my mother's family who visited me, and, who were never frightening to me. In fact, when labouring over my times-tables or mathematics homework my Grandfather, a Cambridge mathematics graduate and lecturer, who had been dead since way before I was born, would often help me with the simple childish sums. This was the house he had lived in while he was growing up, and he was always willing to lend a helping hand.

My two, now deceased, spinster Great Aunts, Lily and Daisy Carter, from whom we bought the house in 1958, often came to sit with me, from spirit, while I was alone in the morning-room painting. Both were artists in their own right and their paintings hung in all rooms of the house. Daisy, during her lifetime, would paint lovely delicate flower paintings in watercolour and ink. She would paint dog roses, irises and lilies on smooth cartridge paper which were signed and dated then placed into gold Victorian frames. Lily, on the other hand painted on canvas, in oil, large landscapes of Yorkshire and some smaller watercolour landscapes now brown-spotted with age.

The family home was named 'Dentdale' acquired from the Cowgill area in the Yorkshire Dales where my ancestors had come from in the seventeenth century. The Carter family bible goes back to 1647 when our ancestors were known as Richard and Isabella Thistlethwayte who were Quakers. It was 2007 when I felt the need to visit the family home in Cowgill where I found that their Quaker church was now a lovely bed and breakfast in which I slept when I stayed in the Dales. I stayed two nights and on the first, as I tried to sleep, I was aware of a young woman in seventeenth century Quaker clothing, very simply clothed and dark haired with a shawl over her shoulders. She entered the room through one wall and out through the wall directly ahead of her through the edge of my bed. The room was as cold as ice and as she emerged from the wall in front of me a cold breeze came with her and left as she disappeared through the wall to the head of my bed. I slept little. I couldn't! It was not fear of another apparition; it was the cold in the room which didn't warm for the rest of my stay. When I had breakfast the owners said that the room I slept in was originally the front door and doorway into the church which made sense of the direction she was walking. They didn't really want a ghost in the house and suggested I took my ancestor home with me. I believe the lady was Alice Thistlethwayte (1680-1750) who together with her husband William (1677-1766) 'walked the length and breadth of Yorkshire, Lancashire and Cheshire teaching their Quaker faith' (information gleaned from part of my cousin's book, *Common Ancestors* by Alan Carter (n.k.). During the same visit I also explored the Thistlethwayte family home in Cowgill which was about a mile along the road from the bed and breakfast and now owned by an artist and her husband who have had other Thistlethwayte family members come to visit from many parts of the world. I felt I had shifted something from my spirit by visiting Dentdale as though one of my ancestors was 'hanging on' until I got there. The Quakers of the time, as part of their religious fervour, shook with the power of the spirit and it seemed right that I should have visited their home in such a beautiful place. I had always had a strange feeling about Alice Thistlethwayte as though she was calling me from afar.

I later found that she and her husband were elders in the Cowgill church and their names have been recorded in my local Quaker church, which was built about 1717. This particular era in my ancestors' history

Later that year I was to leave primary school and resume my education at the local secondary school which was just across the road. My parents had asked the education authority for me to have a place at Roman Catholic grammar school as the three preferred choices, but somehow I was sent to the school which I now know was much better for my future. Being a rather nervous, sensitive child, I realise now that I would not have succeeded as well I as I did in the more competitive environment of Grammar education and I was also glad to be away from the strict religious environment of catholic education. I was a happy child in a simple school rather than a potentially unhappy pupil in a larger less family orientated educational establishment.

I started at Bankfield Secondary Modern School in Tuebrook Liverpool, in September 1961. This was the first time I had not been educated in the same classroom as my twin brother. It was a happy school and I got on very well there. I was always in plays and variety shows and because my PE teacher was Jackie MacDonald, one of the singer, songwriters' from the 1960's 'Jackie and Bridie' (O'Donnall) folk singing duo. In 1963, having been invited by Jackie, I was on BBC TV singing with her on a show called 'Barn Dance'. I remember the song, one composed by Jackie; 'Everybody loves Saturday Night' as clearly as though we sang it yesterday. I was asked to sing a verse alone, and although nervous of the TV cameras and getting the whole thing wrong, I sang in key, loudly and with confidence, and thoroughly enjoyed the whole experience. Jackie and Bridie also had the group of young Bankfield Folk Singers singing at the Liverpool Royal Philharmonic Hall each year for what was then known as 'Commonwealth Day' celebrations. It was also around this time that I became involved with the Liverpool Youth Theatre and the Everyman Youth Theatre and studied filmmaking with Bob Truman and Dave Wade, the tutors.

I understand now how much the learning and experiences I had then has helped me become more confident and able to demonstrate drawings and speak in front of people without being nervous. In 1962 the TV show, 'Barn Dance', singing with my teacher Jackie MacDonald, helped me be confident to work in film and TV shows in my adult life as a Spirit Artist. In 1994 after returning from working in Los Angeles with Pepper Lewis, who channels Gaia, Mother Earth, I was invited by Anglia TV to do an episode of their 'The Something Strange Show' where I drew a portrait, completely away from the audience, of a mother, which was accepted by a lady in the audience and another time HTV invited me to draw a portrait on their 'Magic and Mystery Show' which was also accepted. I feel now that the help and support I received in my secondary school with Miss MacDonald, gave me the extra skills and confidence to stand up in; theatres and Halls, sometimes in front of hundreds of people, television, radio, theatres, community and church halls, which I do now.

The art teacher at Bankfield Girls Secondary Modern School, in Liverpool, was Mrs. Varley who, I believe, was a relation of the artists' John Varley, (1778-1842) and his brother, Cornelius (1791-1873). Mrs. Varley taught me, alongside another 30, or so, pupils in my art lessons, the rudiments of drawing and painting at the school. Although I was never to achieve the accolade of a first prize in art, I would create my homework for Mrs Varley, overestimating my ability and seeing my paintings as masterpieces, in the same room as my Great Aunts' Lily and Daisy from whose paintings I often gained inspiration. Sometimes my drawings were good and sometimes bad, sometimes put on the school-room wall and sometimes hidden from view, but I loved every moment creating them.

When I was thirteen my choice of future career was discussed at the usual careers meeting with the headmistress and a careers officer. When asked what I wanted to do as a career I replied; "A remedial gymnast"! This was quite out of the blue and, to the horror of the Head Mistress, I wanted to help people in hospital with wasting muscles and curved spines. "A remedial gymnast!" retorted Miss Mason the head teacher; "You, my dear, are going to be an Art Teacher". And, so, a self fulfilling prophecy came into play. I became an Art Teacher. I hadn't thought about going against the Head Mistress's suggestion or felt pressured into going into that career choice, it just worked out that way.

Gaining more than enough GCE's and CSE's to be sent to the posh local grammar school up the road at the age of 16 I started my sixth form education at Holly Lodge High School for Girls. I went there to complete my secondary schooling both in education and in learning about boys! I took 'A' level Art and General Studies which I passed which was enough with my previous certificates to apply to Colleges of Further Education. I was driven to my interview in the summer of 1967 by my boyfriend at the time in a bright red MG Midget sports car with the roof down most of the way, and was awarded a place at Matlock College to study art, education and the practice of teaching for three years after which I gained two distinctions in Art and Teaching Practice and a credit in the history of education. These results were enough to be offered a place, with only four other students that year, to study Art Education qualifying at Nottingham University. In just one year of study I gained the degree of Bachelor of Education.

I loved creating art but I also loved teaching and sharing my abilities. After completing my degree in 1972 I was offered a place to teach art and crafts in an American summer camp in New England where I met my lifelong friend Beth. Before leaving England to teach abroad I was unable to secure a teaching job in Liverpool where, after my father had died suddenly the year before, I was expected to return, so on returning from the States I contacted Joe Shirley the art advisor for the employment of Liverpool teachers who said he had lost my application forms. I was horrified! After working so hard at College and gaining a higher degree than most art teachers there may not even be a job for me when the country was crying out for teachers and maybe I should have taken the job I was offered in Derbyshire or even America?

All turned out well because, although I was only a probationary teacher, I was offered the position as Head of Art, which I worked at for eighteen years, in the Toxteth district of Liverpool. I was so happy in my job as an art teacher. I was able to paint, draw and create all day with the some wonderful, lively and often very deprived children in Liverpool. I exhibited their work in the two Liverpool Cathedrals and my own paintings were exhibited independently in country-wide galleries but also as part of the organisation I supported and chaired for a while, the Liverpool Art Teachers Group. It was a very happy time with the art teachers often staying out all night after an Art Teachers meeting chatting and chewing over ideas for weekend retreats in the Lake District and future exhibitions and then going straight into work often without going home. Those were the days of my 'misspent youth' and very exciting ones.

Apart from the artwork I produced in my role as Head of Art for the children in school, I also painted to sell. I painted landscapes and portraits in watercolour on watercolour paper and many, at the exhibitions in the North West of England and Derbyshire, were sold. I did not paint to sell, I would travel out into the Lake District or Wales to sit and draw or photograph, then work on the piece at home. My landscapes were mostly moody in character, rain, snow or heavy grey clouds and rainbows the better. Sometimes I overworked the painting in chalk and charcoal, the watercolours often taking on the dark, rainy quality of Britain itself. Inspired by our local Liverpool art lecturer, Peter Prendergast who, when available, let me use his cottage in Bethesda, North Wales, from where most of the steamy etheric, apparitional landscapes where inspired.

Portraits, on the other hand, were worked either in pencil or charcoal with an almost photographic quality. At the age of 17yrs I painted, in oils on board, my first self-portrait. I remember the evening class art lecturer say to me that I had glamorised myself up a bit, but, I took no notice and still believe, as it hangs on my studio wall, that it was an excellent likeness of me. As the portrait was painted in a more expressionist style, my mother kept it locked away until I recovered it in 2007 when she wasn't looking! Other portraits were of family members and some of African women with beaded necks and hair, finely drawn on heavy white cartridge now yellowed with age. Several were sold to a friend, John Peters, an English Lecturer at Liverpool University, who hung them in his Princes Road flat above his grand piano; a scene from by-gone days.

I exhibited my work in and around Liverpool at the end of the 1970's until the late 1980's when I relocated to Staffordshire. The Bluecoat Gallery was a favourite to exhibit, amongst the Liverpool Galleries, and I also organised several 'one-man' exhibitions in Libraries. Ainsdale and Birkdale in Lancashire were two of the most successful and, in Derbyshire, at my exhibition in St. Michael's Gallery, alongside Derby Cathedral; I sold quite a few paintings. I was definitely not interested in the pomp circumstance and glamour of the wine and cheese openings to my one-man exhibitions, they were just not in my nature, and, I was happy when the sooner the evening was over the better. However, in order to bring the paintings to the notice of the viewer and potential buyer, the procedure had to be tackled. Usually most of the sales were on such evenings and some people would buy two of them to my amazement. I was still under the impression that my drawings on cartridge paper in an oily type of pencil used for drawing on glass. The simply structured artwork, defined by the subtle shading on the cheeks, chin, eyes and hair, would manifest as an Egyptian or Aztec, a spiritual force for the seeker to look to for guidance. Sometimes a family member or friend would make an appearance under the stroke of her pencil on the paper, accompanied by loving words of encouragement or upliftment spoken softly by her. Once I drew a portrait of an artist guide to help me to understand the process of doing this work. I thought of the line drawing as Pierre and when I took it to show Linda she went to her art folder and took out a drawing she had created for me, the novice, and said that the drawing was of Piers, my art guide. Putting the two drawings together we found that they were almost identical. When things happen supernaturally like this some people would say that they were 'spooky', but to Linda and I the hairs went up on our arms, a chill came into the air around us and we remarked at how close the drawings were to each other. I had found my first artist guide!

Watching Linda create these mystical portraits out of nowhere onto blank sheets of paper gave me the impetus to try to draw the portraits for myself. Like Linda I was a reasonably good artist and in my spare time I would start to draw characters of people who I thought maybe in the spirit world. I drew in pencil on cartridge paper the anecdotic faces one after the other. An Egyptian, a Buddhist or Tibetan monk, a gypsy complete with scrying crystal, a magician and a cheeky eyed child were drawn, all competent all picture perfect but how did I know they were spirit portraits drawn from the psychic senses? I didn't, and I could not comprehend why these very good, almost photographic, portraits may not be spirit people. What was it that made a portrait of a person different from a spirit person and what did not? My quest was about to begin.

Later that year, after attending some more of Billy's classes and joining his house circle where the group sat in circle specifically to develop their psychic skills, I found that what I thought of as 'an artist's eye', that is the seeing of people who were not visible to most, was actually a psychic faculty known as clairvoyance. All the time, when I saw people wandering in and out of my bedroom, it was not because I was an artist but because I was a clairvoyant.

The circle was very conveniently held just around the corner from my house and it was always full of people trying to see beyond the mortal world. The meeting was held the same evening, once a week, winter and summer, by invitation only. Like the séances of the past, we were told that the group of people who attended should attend every week, through rain hail or shine, so that the spiritual energies built up in the room would remain constant. And for about a year we all piled into Billy's front room, sitting in the same seat, politely chatting in hushed voices waiting for Billy, the leader, to take his seat.

The impression I had of my first séance was that of reverence to the world with which we were about to commune. I was unusually nervous, but not a going-to-the-dentist type feeling, it was a feeling similar to the excitement one can feel as a thunderstorm approaches. Eighteen men and women were sitting in soft padded Victorian chairs expectantly waiting for the Master to arrive so the psychic show could begin. The lights dimmed and clicked off as a candle was lit in the centre of the room. No table to turn, no hymns sang, no rattling or shaking of the curtains or moveable objects, just a short reverent invocation to the unseen world of spirits to join us with meditation music playing in the background.

Billy Roberts, previously a rock-band member in the 1960's and now a working psychic medium in his own right entered the room, as the lights dimmed and the candle lit, and began the meeting by welcoming everyone to the group. As he mentioned I was a new member I wondered if all newcomers were given the chair by the chill of the door or was it because I arrived slightly late. After the introduction and invitation to the spirit world we were taken into a calming meditation. My mind was all over the place. I was thinking of work, home, whether the cats were in or out and what I should have for dinner the following day. I just couldn't follow his words and when he asked us to count our breath; in two three, out two three, my heart, usually quiet and calm, began to bounce all over the place. I felt as though I was choking as I breathed. Was this really the place for me? Later when the rest of the group, relaxed and calm, 'came back into the room', he asked if everyone could follow his voice. Not wishing to seem ignorant, but being so, I stayed quiet and listened to the others relate their difficulties,

There was one in this circle who I admired a great deal. This was Ged Deacon. He realised I was a novice and that I didn't understand the process and methodology by which the spirit world manifested all that they did, and took me under his wing to show me the way. He was a healer with Billy Roberts and Helen Yaffe, Billy's mother in law. The first time I met him I was in awe of his golden aura. I had never encountered an aura quite so bright and I have never seen one like it again. He took me to the Psychic Truth Centre in the Dingle, Liverpool where I experienced my first Spiritualist service. I was not unaware of the Centre because I had passed the church every day of my teaching life while at St. Winefride's school, but I had never been inside.

The Centre was a typical Victorian building in its own grounds, car park to the side and a large half timbered doorway with porch over the front. A small hallway led into a large hall with what looked like a pulpit, but was actually a fenced platform where the mediums and church officiates sat. On the Sunday afternoon in 1984 when Ged took me to the church for the first time the room was bright with the sun coming through large windows. Light summery church music was being played at the small electric organ by a gentleman whose feet danced on the pedals as his hands deftly touched the keys. The hall was almost empty but for a few elderly ladies dotted about the room, eyes closed, contemplating the music, some whispering the words to the old remembered songs. We sat on blue velvet padded chairs, middle left to the side of the windows. In the short moments that I was in the hall I too was taken, mesmerised by the music, to other times and worlds, swaying slightly to the rhythm of the tunes.

At 3pm precisely the mood changed. An official looking woman walked into the hall with an entourage of followers; a sombre looking man and an elderly lady. Each took their place on the platform, the brisk woman in the centre with the lady and gentleman either side. The congregation stood as the woman walked down the centre aisle. Ged smiled, inviting me to stand. The leader of the group introduced Mary Duffy to be our medium for the afternoon and asked us to sing a hymn, leading on to the medium's prayer, and then the 'The Lord's Prayer', which would be sung. Reminiscences of previous church services came to mind as a short healing hymn was sung. Mary Duffy, a dark haired Scottish voiced lady, stood, eyes closed, to speak a prayer inviting the spirit world to join us on our quest for spiritual knowledge.

The prayer was long and drawn-out but could be followed easily as an invocation for us to join our hearts with the unseen world, which she said it was all about us. Still standing we were asked to be quiet for one minute to send our love and thoughts out to those who needed healing. This was followed by the Lord's Prayer. Fortunately having been in the school choir I was able to sing to the 23rd psalm easily and I thoroughly enjoyed the memory, taking me back to my school days when I was able to sing the hymn in three part harmony.

The rousing prayer seemed to lift the spirits of those present, after which the congregation sat and noisily replaced the hymnbooks in the pocket to the back of the chair in front of them. It was time for the rather sombre man to give his philosophy of the day. Having never come across a service like this before I was rather taken aback by the relaxed manner these non-ordained people had. His philosophy was dry, preaching with lack of humour or intonation in his voice, that the spirit world is all around us and whether we are good or bad we all would eventually go there. The lecture lasted about 20 minutes, reminding me of the Roman Catholic Sunday sermon when the children would become restless and start to kick the bottom of the kneeling board below their feet. Ged smiled at me again but this time lifted his eyebrows, suggesting he was feeling the same.

Another hymn was sung, this time 'Abide with Me' as a monetary offering was taken. Feeling embarrassed because I was not aware the plate was to be handed around the hall, Ged thrust a few coins into my hand to place into the velvet-green padded wooden dish as it was handed to me. The congregation hushed in expectancy as the medium Mary Duffy stood and cleared her throat. Many years later I became aware that Mrs Duffy was known as one of the finest mediums in the world and so due respect was given at her services if you were lucky enough to get a seat at one.

She began by explaining that she was just about to communicate with the spirit world and that there would be a verbal message from them to someone in the room. She asked that if it seemed the message was for someone in the room, to speak out clearly so she could use the voice as a communication tool with those in spirit. "I have a Bill here looking for his daughter." There was silence. "I have a gentleman called William or Bill who passed to the world of spirit with a heart condition who is looking for his daughter." My heart began to pound! Does my father want to speak to me, I asked myself? Ged looked at me and said, "Say yes" which I did. Mrs Duffy repeated to me what she had just said and asked me if I understood what she was saying. I said, 'Yes I did.'

People turned to look at me. I was embarrassed, heart pounding and I was feeling very hot all of a sudden.

"Is this your father?" she said.

"Yes it is," I replied. Then followed a message from someone in the spirit world who could have been my father but it could also have been his father or indeed an uncle because they were all called William, however only one died with a heart condition. I didn't wish to complicate matters by saying this and the message turned out to be an integral point to my understanding of why I had been taken to that church on that day.

The message, which was directed specifically to me from the medium, was to tell me to use my capacity and skill as an artist, as a form of mediumship called spirit art. Later I found out that Mrs Duffy worked in tandem with another, very famous, spirit artist called Coral Polge, so the message was even more poignant when I spoke, many years later, to Coral, making the point that when she retired there would be a need for someone else to draw the spirit world. Ged was pleased I had received a verbal message from my Dad which was the first and the last I received. Later that day I tried to do a drawing for Ged but it was not conclusive enough for me to accept that I was reaching out into the world of spirit.

Ged took me to many psychic services both in the Psychic Truth Centre, where I met up with the medium Tommy Richardson who would prove very important to my spiritual development a few years later, and the other Liverpool Spiritualist Church in Daulby Street where I was later married in 1988. Ged and I were invited to sit in a circle of people who lived not too far from my home in Newcastle Road, Wavertree. The house, we were invited to, was a small red brick Victorian terraced house just off Penny Lane. The séance was what is known as a physical circle whereby the spirit world could, if ectoplasm was built up enough, manifest 'physically' in the room with us. The group of people were psychic enthusiasts who were not involved with any churches or spiritualist activities. They believed that the spirit of a living being or animal survived physical death. It was the first time I had been invited to such a serious group and because it was serious we had to attend every meeting and be exactly on time. There was a belief that the spirit world had made an appointment with us and they had built up the energy specifically to be used so they could be felt, heard or seen with the physical eye which is very different from clairvoyance which is an inner sight. Having had some experiences of ectoplasm as a child and at Linda's circle I was not too worried about the outcome of the séance, and anyway I was in Ged's safe hands and he seemed to know what he was doing.

The first evening we arrived at the appointed hour. It was September and the nights were drawing in after the long hot summer, the evening was cold with an easterly wind just catching us as we walked to the house. The gentleman who invited us opened the front door and we were led straight into a room with no carpet, curtains or furniture, just a table in the middle of the room with six chairs. The window was boarded and although there was an electric light and fire switched on when we arrived as soon as the séance began both were switched off. The kitchen led off from this room but a double door stopped any light or sound from entering the room.

There were already several people in the room who we did not know and we were shown where to sit. I was placed to the left of Ged who was at the head of the table opposite our host. It was our first session and I was apprehensive, not knowing what to expect. The grandmother clock in the hallway struck seven thirty and the lights and fire were switched off. Total blackness hit me. No light greeted my senses, just the sound of breathing from other members of the group. There was no agenda to the evening which we knew about, except in opening the séance our host began singing a popular, but old fashioned song, 'Roll out the Barrel', aided by the others in the group. Then silence! I closed my eyes to see if it was just as dark inside my head as outside and it was! However that was just about to change because in front of me I began to see an undeterminable shape, that I assumed was directly in front of me. I closed my eyes and the shape disappeared, opened them, and the shape appeared but slightly larger. As I watched the swirls of the shape I noticed that the centre of the shape was building into a pulsating blue/silver light almost the size of a fist, that is, if in case the whole magical experience ended. We looked towards Ged and as we did so a small star-like-light broke away from the vision towards his head. As it did so I noticed a movement in his auric field as though his golden aura was shifting away from his body towards the star.

Ged's intrinsic panic energy was always good. He seemed so positive about where he was going and what he was to do. He had placed a large red ring around the 29th November, a date on his calendar in his living room. He said that that day would be a 'red letter' day for him and his life would start to move again. Always thinking of others, he would help people whether he knew them or not, but tonight his energy, his life force, glowed brighter than usual. All those who could see his life force were in awe of the magnificence of it. As soon as the star touched Ged's glowing aura the light-show disappeared completely. Not a wisp to be seen, not even of the aura it touched. The room seemed warmer and calmer, my heart beat began to slow from the beating it was having during the event and, as our host became more aware of the loss of the supernatural being, he ended the séance.

Little was discussed within the group but Ged and I spent hours chatting about the event with friends and family, neither of us knowing what the experience was about. Very little happened over the next few weeks in the circle, it was as though the spirit world had used up three weeks' worth of energy on that night. Although we did not want to miss the circle on the 29th November we both had tickets to attend the Psychic Evening to be held at Woolton Hall Hotel that evening. I was to drive three friends and Ged was to make his own way there. Linda and Les, old friends of Ged's, were with me in the car and we were looking forward to watching Billy Roberts, Mavis Patila, Sue Rowland, Jill Harland and a few of our friends demonstrating mediumship from the stage. Billy organised a few of the events a year and Ged always helped out at the door.

It was particularly cold, wet and unusually dark that night driving to Woolton Hall. It is particularly difficult to see the entrance to the drive and that night, with the driving rain, it was worse than usual. I missed the entrance and couldn't turn the car around to go back, for a few miles. We were running late as it was and having to drive those few extra miles made us even later. When we eventually arrived at the Hall there was an ambulance in front of the entrance. We all wondered what had happened, was someone ill? Billy was standing at the entrance like a small black shadow against the light. He said quietly, "It's Ged, he's had a heart attack, someone needs to go with him!"

Les and I got into the back of the ambulance. I had parked my car under a tree at the back of the Hall and hoped it would be all right. I held Ged's hand as we sped to the Hospital, lights and alarm bells ringing both outside and inside my head. Reminiscences of my father flooded into my mind. His hand was clammy but I spoke to him all the way giving him verbal and emotional encouragement that he would be all right. Five minutes after he was taken into the accident and emergency ward a white coated gentleman said that Ged had been pronounced dead on arrival.

I reflected on what happened in the circle and on the 29th November many times after that. I didn't sit in séance with the group again and I didn't attend any more workshops or demonstrations. It is my belief that just as we are not meant to know the date of our birth nor do we know the date of our death. If we did we may want to cheat the 'grim reaper'. But why did Ged know something was to happen on the 29th and why did the 'angel of death' visit us in that group that night? Sometimes life is so complicated and difficult to understand logically but my recollection of that night in the séance room with Ged will never be forgotten. It was almost as though the spirit world was preparing for his passage home to the world where we all belong, away from the theatre '... the slings and arrows of outrageous fortune' and the physical world of the earth. Ged remains as a strong guiding force around me as I demonstrate my spiritual work. He promised to look after me in life and his spirit has not broken that promise to this day.

I remained a school teacher alongside my spiritual work but as I began the study of psychic phenomena within the Spiritualist Church and the Spiritualist National Union (SNU), it was not looked highly upon by the catholic school and my work colleagues. I was still a Head of Art at St. Mary's High School, Toxteth, but when I spoke to one of my art teachers, Ken Lesser, who said I shouldn't get involved with people who talk and communicate with the dead, I was upset because I looked upon Ken as having good judgement. I was quite confused by his comment because he was a Freemason and I couldn't quite understand the difference between communication with the spirit world and some of the properties Freemasonry has within its practice and initiation. I began to learn not to speak about my not-so-new beliefs and experiences at work which seemed to help matters there a great deal. Seeing and speaking to the invisible can unnerve many people even though parapsychologist's and transpersonal psychologist's have been researching spirit communications scientifically for many years.

However, my study of spiritualism began with a SNU written postal course my tutor being Eric Hatton who was, at that time, the President of the Union. The SNU postal course spilled over onto a course in 'Understanding Mediumship' at Daulby Street Spiritualist Church where I learnt, amongst other things, that I had been a medium all my life, but also, now was the time to put my mediumship into practice. It was at Daulby Street that I learnt how the spirit world communicated with us, why they communicated with us and the responsibilities which came with giving messages from the so-called dead to the living. I was given a chance to hear direct voice phenomenon performed at the church and watch a light- weight silver trumpet lift from a table with no-one touching it. It was at Daulby Street Spiritualist Church where I learnt 'my trade' as a medium. Although I was born a medium and spent most of my early life seeing, speaking to and trying to avoid the ones who were not my family of friends, I still had to learn that we are all spirit in the here and now. I had to learn that the only difference between the spirit world and here is the fact that in the physical world we have a solid, physical body. It is as simple as that! WE ARE ALL SPIRIT NOW!

I began working as a novice medium demonstrating platform mediumship in the Spiritualist churches, under the fine tutelage of Glynn Edwards, an international medium and tutor at the Arthur Findlay College. I was clueless of how to start because I had never had any instruction on the techniques, methodology and process of mediumship but Glyn and the other tutors were very understanding and supportive. It was during one of these Wednesday night classes that it came out that I was an artist and Glyn started me off with some spirit art sketches. These sketches were very basic at first but as the evidence of who the spirit person was in the drawing, together with recognition by the recipient, I gained in confidence. Those times of struggling and of not knowing if the portrait had been influenced by me or the spirit world began to disappear. I was getting to know the sensations of when the spirit presence was with me and when it was not. Glyn, during our sessions as novices would always say; "Question everything! Not everyone in the spirit world is goodness and light." Years later I would find this to be too true when completing a drawing during a spirit art demonstration and a deceased prisoner from Her Majesty's jail came through. An inveterate liar everything he said had to be taken with a pinch of salt! But a lady took the drawing with thanks, she knew who he was and at that time her son had been up before the magistrate so she also was aware of why he had come to her.

I did not have to learn how to draw a portrait because I already had the ability to do that with my art training but to put both the art and the mediumship together was a different story. For the first few years of demonstrating spirit art I worked with a medium that would make a link with the drawing and the recipient. Even though I was a medium myself it was difficult at first to draw and make the appropriate link with the clairaudient part of my work. The medium would either make the link with the spirit world while I am drawing, or, link into my drawing and then make a connection with the recipient of the message. Sometimes this worked and sometimes it didn't, but I soon learnt that the auric energy of the medium had to be similar to mine before the drawing would be successful. If the medium was very dominant the coming together of the drawing and message did not generally work with their link in the audience. Similarly, if I was too dominant, the message giving was not successful. However, when I worked with two mediums in particular the artwork and message seemed to flow more naturally. These mediums were Tommy Richards from the Psychic Truth Centre and Tony Gleeson from Preston Spiritualist Church. Tommy used to call himself 'the reluctant medium' because he never wanted to be a medium; he said it was thrust upon him. Tony, on the other hand was an SNU trained medium who in later years named my newborn daughter at Wolverhampton Spiritualist Church. Although the two mediums were like chalk and cheese I was able to work with both of them easily when drawing the spirit world.

In the late 1980's I relocated from Liverpool to the Midlands and having suffered severe back problems from giving birth to my daughter at the age of 40 I missed working with my two friends when working with spirit. Tommy died shortly after I moved and was a sad loss to both mediumship and the spirit world. Tony still works from the spiritualist podium but I didn't work with him again. He was kind enough to introduce me to several Spiritualist churches before I moved house, one of which was Wolverhampton SNU Church where I worked for over twenty years demonstrating, teaching and working with psychic and spirit art with the local people and members of the church.

My journey into making the connection between the two abilities I was born with, art and mediumship may seem to have been a long one, and to some perhaps it has been. However, the path I chose to take has been deliberately slow and careful enabling me to enjoy fully what I experienced with and from the spirit world. It is so easy to fall into the trap of being told by a medium that we have this that and the other spiritual gift and off we go producing seemingly spirit portraits with no concrete evidence, which I feel is a danger to both the novice and to an unsuspecting recipient.

Billy Roberts once said to me that if I developed my skills too quickly I could 'burn out'. Too many times I have seen this happen when I have come across the novice studying mediumship. I feel it is my responsibility to teach what I know slowly and responsibly. I am aware I am working with the vulnerable psyche of a student and have taken the time to train and help those wishing to study spirit and psychic art. Part of the degree I took whilst at teacher training college was in behavioural psychology which helps me understand how people learn and understand what they are studying. I have also taken a course in hypnotherapy and Neurolinguistic Programming (NLP) which gives me an idea of problems people can have while learning mediumship and how to overcome them. During my teaching career I have gained skills in the understanding of how people learn and how they assimilate knowledge. Do you know if you are a visual, auditory or kinaesthetic learner? Well, when teaching workshops and groups of people who have been out of education, some for a long time, it is vitally important, especially lecturing on the invisible skills of mediumship, to understand the way different people learn. We are all different.

It is also very important to be able to say to people, who may be struggling with seeing, sensing or hearing the spirit world that the place they are going to in their mind may not be where they think they are, and not to give people false hope. I cannot stress here how important it is to develop the skills slowly so the learning can 'sit in' accurately. Mediumship, when developed too fast, can, in some cases, cause health problems. I do believe that everyone has the potential to be a spiritual medium, some just don't want to be and abhor the idea of speaking to the spirit of someone whose has died, some are better making a psychic connection with the in-built spirit and linking into the earth energies within the aura of a person, and some are born with the ability to communicate with the spirits of the dead and know that this ability is to be used to help people and can be a vocation.

I now realise that, although I was born with the facility to communicate with the spirit world, it was not until I was secure in my job and a mature adult that the right people and situations had to come along for me to understand the process I was to teach later in life. Only then did I begin creating and manifesting the paranormal art works and messages. Understanding the process by which the spirit communicates, and the methods which can be utilised, is an integral part of the manifestation of any mediumship and the learning process cannot be taken for granted. Those novices who have come to me through the churches or workshops, organised by others in many lands in the world, have been given the skills to match their abilities. Many have successfully gone on to produce spirit portraits at demonstrations of spirit art and others to develop their skills as artists in their own right. I teach spirit art so that others can go and demonstrate the skill. I do not believe it should be considered 'just another form of mediumship'. A portrait with verbal evidence can give that ultimate evidence which can be recognised by the ones who loved them while on earth. It is not about showmanship it is about evidence. That is; the evidence that our spirit survives physical death.

SPIRIT SKETCHES AND PORTRAIT STUDIES

Chapter Four

WHAT IS SPIRIT?

What is the point in writing a book about portraits of the deceased which have been influenced or been drawn by the deceased? In western society we often think, and have been influenced to think in this way by religious doctrines, that we should never contact the dead or make the first move towards communication with spirit world or the world of the dead. However, those of us who are spiritual mediums could not get very far without a communicator in the invisible-to-most other world making contact with us! I could never understand why people have said that I shouldn't contact the dead, because the contacts I see and hear in the spirit world are all around me and these people don't just mysteriously pop up and say hello; they are there all the time!

I understand what is happening to be like this; we, who are living and are having a physical existence, are space and time sharing with our physically dead friends, family, neighbours and animals. I know that statement, for some, may sound strange, and even rude, but to me, mediumship is all about the symbiotic relationship we, and those who have already shed their mortal suit, have with other dimensions, vibrations and realities. Science is now proving that there is more beyond our physical existence and I am sure that sooner or later hat proof will be available for all to see and understand.

Ideally, our communication between the two worlds should be of mutual consent and respect because when the person in spirit knows they can communicate with us they can be so desperate to get through they are sometimes so desperate they will try anything. They may try to use the latent energy around us to move objects, make the room feel chilled, or create banging and rapping on the walls, TV or furniture, which can scare us if we do not know what is happening. The longer the person remains on the lower levels of psychic and spiritual energy in the spirit world, by desperately wanting to communicate with their loved ones still alive, the less likely they are to want to move on into the lighter areas of the afterlife, of which there are many in God's house. The lower levels are heavier in energy vibration, and more like the physical world, which is why those who are missing the person's physical presence or grieving for the loss of their loved ones are more reluctant to move into the lighter energy vibrations. Also, if we are grieving for them we may be holding them back from the lighter energies in other vibrations of spirit, we should 'let them go' once they have made their presence felt.

So, you have 'popped our clogs', 'croaked it', 'passed over', 'returned to your maker', or just plain 'died' and you are missing those you love and you want to make some sort of a sign that you are 'Still alive and kicking!' What would you do? You might scream and shout in order to attract your family's attention. But those actions no longer work; the people you are trying to attract in the physical world can't hear you. They might feel a chill whenever you come near or you move close to them but unless you are aware of how to communicate through the medium of thought then you may find it difficult to get them to notice you.

The spirit world is all about energies and vibration. When we boil a kettle it changes from water, a heavy solid liquid, to steam, an etheric, almost invisible, disappearing substance. The metamorphosis between water and steam is very similar to the process of moving from the physical world to that of spirit. Once the steam has cooled, which is analogous to the spirit getting used to the spirit world, it returns to a more solid substance, that of water From the spirit side of life, when your physical friend comes close to you, you might notice that the light surrounding them is dull, sometimes duller than at other times. Sometimes you can't see them because they have this dark auric fog around them like a lamp on a misty night. What do you think that is? It can be negative energy from the emotion of grief, because they are missing you, which can be clouding the aura of the person thus making it difficult for the spirit person to make a connection with their friend.

When we are alive we have an aura around us which is controlled by the way we think, the way we feel, physically and emotionally and the how our mental wellbeing is at the time. The aura (different from an 'aura' which people who are epileptic may get before a fit) is an electromagnetic energy surrounding us which can be affected by the aura of others, our surroundings at home and work, our love life and all of the other things which are going on at the time, including the death of a loved one.

When we are born we have a very delicate aura which changes as our mind, emotions and physical body begins to develop and think for ourselves or analyse the objects or people around us. It is well known amongst healers and psychics that the brighter the aura a person has the healthier they are. A person's aura has several intermingling layers to it ranging from the mental/emotional state of the person to their spirituality, and when a psychic or medium 'reads' an aura of a human being or animal (and sometimes rocks, crystals or plants) they 'see' or 'sense' the life force of that individual, animal, material or vegetable.

It is by contacting the spiritual aura that a medium can sense the energies of people who have died and this contact may make the hairs on the back of your neck stand up when a deceased person's spirit energy comes close to you, that's how a medium feels, sees or hears spirit. The spirit of the deceased comes close to us and it is through the mediums' spirit aura, housed in the physical body while alive, which will have a sensation of a *knowing* that a spirit person is close to them, then the medium will decide to ignore or speak to them with their thoughts.

Yes, the medium decides! Not the spirit person! Making a connection with the spirit world is of mutual consent not a one way process. I remember an encounter with a friend's elderly brother who had been in spirit a short time. The gentleman, in life, decided he didn't like me and told his sister that I was not good company to keep because I was a psychic. When he died he tried to speak to his sister through me and I refused to relay the message because while he was alive he didn't like what I did and I felt he had to apologize first before I would give a message to her. Some may think this is rude thing to do, but, although he had never said nasty things to my face, he did to his sister who was my friend, so if he was still alive he would not have wanted to speak to me, so, why in death? I did eventually relay the message, and he did apologise.

So, let's take you, the reader as an example; you have died and your spirit has managed to find its way to your loved ones. Let me explain. The world of spirit is a world of thought. You no longer have a body to walk you from one room into another which means you have to learn how to make a connection, with your loved ones in the physical world. This you will be able to do by using telepathy or the energy of thought to bring about a sensation, an image or a thought. Now, the reason why many people try to, or want to, get a message to their loved ones through a medium is because they don't know how to do it themselves. It is not as simple as tapping someone on the shoulder and saying "hello", even some mediums when they die find it difficult because the earth vibration of energy is lower than the spiritual. And, the deceased person also has to find a medium with the right spiritual energy level for them to communicate through. It is common for a person who was a devout Roman Catholic while alive to wait for a medium with similar spiritual leanings. Or a University Professor with a high level of academic thought to look for the medium who is academic which has happened to me several times. We hear the phrase, 'Let them rest in peace', well, some spirit people may not be able to rest for several reasons. They may have died suddenly without telling anyone where their will was hidden, or they didn't have time to tell their wife they loved them or they were rushing to get to work and, in the spirit world, are still trying to get there. It is after they have done what they needed to do they can then rest and this is as individual to each soul as it is to each medium.

Painting portraits of the dead? Well, not exactly, when asked if I believed in the concept of life after death I replied "No, I do not *believe* that there is a life after death, I *know* that there is a life after death". Once, when being filmed for the television programme *The Something Strange Show* in

Northampton, England, I was told by the production manager that I was a freak. I asked, "Why", and he said that anyone who was so preoccupied by death and the dead must be a freak!

At the end of the show, after I had drawn a portrait of a woman and given verbal evidence to the recipient of the portrait whilst I was held in an interviewing room away from the audience, the producer apologised and said that I must truly be communicating with the spirit world to produce a portrait of a woman's mother without having previously met her. I just remarked, "That's what I do". After I had produced the drawing a TV monitor was switched on for me to scan the audience and I was asked who the drawing was for. I pointed to a lady towards the front of the hall and said that the drawing was her mother. The interviewer asked how I knew and I said a lady was standing with the lady as I drew her and she said she was her mother.

The drawing was taken into the audience by the interviewer and it was explained how I had created it. He then went to the lady I had pointed to and asked do you know who this lady is and she said yes it was her mother. He then asked how did she know and she said I should know my mother but I have a photograph just like the drawing in my bag. She retrieved the photograph and as the drawing was put against the photograph there was a gasp from the audience because the drawing so closely resembled the mother.

The verbal information I gave with the drawing, known as the evidence from spirit, was read out and the lady said that the drawing was accurate. She was given the drawing and I was led into the hall to overwhelming applause. I was shocked myself that the drawing was so like the photo of the mother because most of the time when I draw spirit portraits I cannot 'see' who I am drawing. I just draw what I sense. Another well known medium, Stephen O'Brien, who had also been isolated from the audience, was invited in to the hall and, astonishingly, went straight to the same lady and said, "Your mother is standing very close to you…" which was amazing evidence for those who do not understand the process of mediumship.

I was invited to draw a spirit portrait on another TV show down in Cardiff by HTV for the *Magic and Mystery Show*. For this show I was placed on the stage to draw in front of the audience. I was asked to sit at a table and draw while the show was recorded in 'real time'. The stage was a typical stage set for 'spooky' type films. The production manager had set the scene with lit candles and Victorian furniture, ancient fake paintings above a fireplace, like a set out of a horror movie. This set was a very small part of a very large very cold building which looked and felt like the inside of an airline hanger. It was very interesting to see how the illusion of TV was constructed for people watching to believe we were really in someone's house.

As I was drawing the spirit portrait which I was contracted to do by HTV, other mediums were being interviewed, one of which was Doris Collins. Eventually the TV host, who had introduced me at the top of the show, came to me to look at the drawing. He asked me how I had created the portrait, had I seen the spirit or felt it and why I had created a portrait of a dead person. I gave him the same information in the same way as I had on the other show, but this time he asked me to say who the drawing was for in the audience. I pointed up to the right top row of the auditorium to a young gentleman who was rather shocked I should speak to him. The cameras panned to him as he straightened up in his metal framed chair. He asked, "You mean me?" I said, "Yes, you", and gave him the information which I had received clairaudiently as I was drawing. The portrait was of a young sandy haired man who had passed tragically in a motorbike accident in the 1980's. The gentleman, who was the recipient of the drawing, was obviously shocked and embarrassed to have been picked, remarked to me later that he was not there for a message he just wanted to be on TV, he also said that he did have a friend who had died at that time and who did drive a motorbike but he did not know the particulars of his passing. Later he said that he had stage shock and couldn't think back because of the TV cameras, but he could take the drawing and wanted to ask why his friend had come to see him today. That part is confidential and won't be written here.

These are just two of the many examples I could tell you about from the thousands of drawings and paintings I have created over the years, now worldwide, and am going to create until I eventually join the people I draw. I am going to continue this chapter by choosing a few more of the spirit artworks which had such an impact on the lives of the people who received them. However, before I do that I will give you some examples of how I enable the spirit world to create the art works through me, and, the impact the drawings make on people who receive these works of paranormal art.

I draw and paint in many different ways for different purposes, and, I use different art materials depending on whether I am demonstrating the art to the public at large gathering, creating for a private or postal reading or just working for myself producing artworks which are to be exhibited in art galleries. All methods are very easy for me to create now I have been using them for years, but the process is quite difficult to explain especially if the reader is not a psychic or an artist and not used to psychic or spiritualist jargon. I will try to explain the process as though I am speaking to someone who is interested in mediumship but may not know the art techniques and/or processes I refer to. I shall try to make the explanation of the artistic and psychic techniques as simple as possible with an explanation of what I do in creating a spirit portrait and after that I will give you some examples.

Chapter Five

HOW I CREATE SPIRIT PORTRAITS

My confidence in drawing spirit portraits grew once my spirit portraits and drawings were being confirmed as being the portrait of someone who I had never met and did not know. I began to wonder why I was being inspired to create such unusual images. I was reminded of a summer holiday my daughter and I had on the Isle of Wight when she was very young. I was visiting a lady who was very interested in my art work and I took the opportunity to see her and take a holiday at the same time. It was on my visit to Queen Victoria's summer residence on the Isle of Wight that I began to understand a little more about the artistic inspirations I was receiving from another world. My daughter and I looked around Osborne House and I became very interested in one particular painting. It was situated in a sort of alcove in the corner of one of the upstairs rooms. The painting was a death bed portrait of Queen Victoria. I can't remember who the artist was or when it was painted but I thought it was a strange subject for a painting, and yet some people think that painting portraits of the spirit of those who have died is also strange.

The painting of the cold, still, dead flesh still sends a shiver down my spine, reminiscent of some of the medieval and Victorian statues in churches and graveyards. The painting was masterfully executed with the body of Queen Victoria looking as though she was asleep, head flat upon the pillow, eyes closed with fine white see-through gauze covering her face, at peace at last. The thought, however, running through my head was 'Who on earth would want to draw portraits of the dead!' And yet, many have thought that this is exactly what I do. Moreover, I am often asked if I am frightened of drawing dead people. Let me explain; to me I am not drawing the flesh and blood of the person, the mortal body, like the painting of Queen Victoria, I am drawing a replica of the spiritual persona of the person together with the mask of their mortal body and memories of objects and places they lived. I am drawing the elements of the person and memories they had of themselves, of what they remember about their lives and the people who were important to them in life, which is sent to me as thought impressions which I then draw.

The paranormal experiences I have had since birth have built up tools in my spiritual toolbox, and, it is these tools which enable me to understand the workings of the spirit but also be able to draw and paint the portraits of those in spirit. My spirit mind is able to communicate to those still living as well as those who have moved on into the afterlife. My mind does not have to wait until my body is dead to communicate with other minds in this or other spirit dimensions. Not only do I believe as human beings we can communicate mind to mind before death, animals are able to communicate with us as well, and many of us will experience mind to mind communication at some time during our physical time here on the earth.

Our spirit is communicating *here and now*, not just when we die. Spirit art is created with that in mind so that we can understand the difference between psychic and spirit art. I do not send out a thought to spirit or call the spirits of the dead to me, my spirit mind is constantly in dialogue with the invisible (to most) world of spirit. My spirit can *see* the spirit people and so can utilise my physical body to draw or paint what my spirit sees. My physical eyes do not need to see the face of the spirit person in order to draw the image, I can leave that work up to my spirit, or my spirit guide, to instigate and complete the drawing or any other type of artwork my physical body already knows how to create.

So, this is how I work as a spirit artist. I allow my physical body and brain to gather information from my spirit or spirit mind and then commit the impression to paper or canvas. There is nothing spooky or frightening about what I do, it is all quite simple. And for those who say I am calling to the dead or, "Let the dead rest in peace" I say; "How can this be? My spirit is as alive as it will ever be at the *same time* as my physical body is living, I don't have to be dead to be able to access my spirit."

Of course, the explanation above may seem, to some, as though I have two minds or a split personality, but I assure you my spirit mind and physical brain work hand in hand giving me the ability to operate as is a mediums between two modes of existence commonly known as *the two worlds*. Those whose spirit mind and physical body are not working together or in sync may never have a psychic or spiritual experience in the whole of their physical lifetime which will probably not bother them at all. There will also be those who are on a spiritual path, delving into many church or spiritual experiences, only to receive other- world communication haphazardly. What does understanding the concept of mediumship and why does it matter? We are all here in a physical body for a reason and that reason may not involve mediumship but will involve caring for others and helping others in some another way. Mediumship is not an end in itself; it is the beginning of a journey into the philosophy and meaning of life in the physical world, and it is a fallacy that it is only trained mediums that are mediumistic.

As an example, of certain people having the ability but not wanting the experience to go with it, my mother would say that she is neither a psychic nor a medium but, as a nurse, she was somehow able to name the illness a person in hospital would be suffering from before the doctor had the test results. The doctors would come to her, especially during war-time, to ask her what illness she thought the patient had, and, even though she was right all the time, and knew she had the ability, she did not want to use it. Similarly, her father, my grandfather, a mathematics graduate from Cambridge University, could give predictions about the weather. The Yorkshire farmers would come to him at harvesting time and he would tell them when the best weather would be to bring in the harvest. I have friends who know who is going to be on the phone when it rings. This sort of mediumship I am speaking about. It is not only experienced by mediums but also by ordinary people in the street. These people do not call themselves mediums but they are still communicating with an energy which is outside of and something different from themselves. That's all there is to it!

What are spirit portraits and what is the point in creating them? In my experience as a spirit artist I have come to the conclusion that there are as many different varieties and types of spirit and psychic art as there are artists and mediums. Just as those who compose and produce music are different from each other, and traditional artists creating artworks use different techniques in art process and material, spirit artists do the same. However, to simplify the methodology by which the art is created, I have written about the two major classifications of mediumistic art, that of spirit and psychic art, and how they are mediumistically and artistically mastered into form. Although my main purpose in writing the book is to help others understand the evidential properties of spirit art and the information below is primarily based on spirit art, I still feel that there is a need to discuss the properties of psychic art later, in the book, so that the artist, when working with the energies of spirit, is able to differentiate between the two.

The information below relates to spirit portraiture. When drawing spirit portraits there are three distinct methods of producing the spirit faces;

1. By *sensing* the spirit person to be drawn using, clairaudience or clairsentience (hearing or sensing colours, emotions, names etc)
2. By *amanuensis*, that is, by allowing a spirit artist to draw the images automatically by utilising the physical hand to draw the image usually known as automatic drawing
3. By psychically *seeing* the person subjectively and objectively with the 'inner eye' or physical eye, and then, by using artistic abilities, draw the spirit person as you would a still life or life drawing.

Spirit art can be drawn in a variety of venues. The usual places in which I have created spirit portraits in the past are;

*   At public demonstrations either in private homes, church halls, theatres, TV studios, community centres where I would be

presented in front of the public who would expect me to produce a spirit portrait with verbal evidence

+ At private sittings either in my studio, Spiritualist church meetings or people's homes. A private sitting is when an enquirer will come to see me confidentially and expect a drawing of a loved one or guide with verbal evidence

+ A postal or email reading which is usually when people can't visit me for a one-to-one session because they may live in another country, it is too far for them to travel or they cannot come to me for other reasons. I will create one or more drawings without having met them and then post the drawing or painting together with information about the picture. An email reading is similar except I will photograph the image and send it down-line with a written reading. I would usually post the portrait to them as well.

If I see a spirit figure manifest in my home or studio I am able, by virtue of already being an artist, to draw the person as though they are sitting for me in life. These paintings are usually of people who have come to help me in some way or other. I have seen several solid spirit people who I have gone on to paint on canvas in acrylic paint which I have then exhibited in art shows.

The art process of painting or drawing a spirit portrait is the same as when I am drawing any other drawing. I use the same materials, usually pastel, pencil, watercolour paint with wax crayons or acrylic paint on paper, board or canvas depending on what and who I am creating the image for. If the work is for a commission or for an exhibition I will paint in acrylic on canvas, if the image is for a private reading it will generally be produced on white or coloured paper using pencil, pastel or watercolour paint, and, if I am giving a public demonstration of spirit art I will work in pastel or conte crayon on flip chart paper.

As well as the art materials, which are used in the making of these paranormally produced artworks, I must not forget to mention the psychic energy which has to be present when making the psychic and spirit art, because without the paranormal energies the drawings would just be ordinary portraits. The spirit energies may be in the form of a spirit artist who wishes to draw for me, or the supernaturally produced ectoplasm which moulds the solid spirit form which builds up the solid-like manifestation of a person who has lived and died. To those of you who do not consider yourself mediumistic and who say you cannot 'see' the spirit world, many spirit artists 'feel' the sensations of the portrait. This all may seem strange to a person who is not mediumistic, but, the student may *feel* the colour red or the colour of the spirit person's eyes. They do not see the clear blue of the eye of the spirit person, they will sense it. When I am teaching how to produce spirit drawings I start my students off with drawing sensations rather than what they can see because there are very few spirit artists who actually see the image of the spirit world in front of them.

A very wonderful psychic artist, who I met several times, was Coral Polge. She states, in her book *Living Images* that she was clairsentient, that is, she drew, most of the time, impressions she felt as a medium and not what she saw as an artist. On the other hand, Frank Leah said he saw clairvoyantly and drew who he saw. As an artist I create my own portraits in all ways, feeling the presence, sensing the impressions of height, weight or whiskers, seeing the face directly in front of me or subjectively in my 'mind's eye'. I use all ways so that the image of the spirit person can be as accurate as possible. You may ask, for what reason? Those who have received drawings or paintings of their loved ones are grateful to know that their family or friends are 'safe' and that they can move on in their lives with the knowledge that there is someone looking after them. Not to predict the future but to love and guide them in their times of stress and or happiness.

I can understand the concern of those who have lost their family or friend suddenly who hope, (because they have seen films and TV programmes about 'lost souls' and 'ghosts'), that their people in spirit are OK, and I have been told by people who have received a drawing that the solid impression on paper is absolute proof that their loved one is there in the spirit world. Then they can 'let go' to allow the spirit to move on in the spirit world and not be stuck in the heavy materialistic essence of physical existence. We should let them go in order for them to progress in the lighter brighter happier existence of the world of love and not continuously demand their presence close to us. It is our duty to allow them to progress to the place where their spirit or soul can learn and progress, we are doing them an injustice to continually want them with us. Once drawn, and the understanding that their spirit has survived mortal death, let them go, give them the chance to move on in the world which is more our home than here in the physical existence.

We know it is possible for the dead to communicate with us using the medium of thought, we have known that for centuries. However, there are many do not believe there is an after-life and, equally others who do not want to consider the thought of it because of moral or religious grounds. As an educationalist I was unable to talk about my spirit work and can understand the fear or reluctance in others and I would not like to offend or force my beliefs onto others who have very different beliefs, perhaps only considering mediums as fortune-tellers and have little time for them. I encountered this not so long ago at an Art Lecturers meeting when I was asked what sort of art work I was exhibiting locally. It was at the time when the Spirit Art Society was showing spirit art work in a local gallery. So I said to the enquirers, 'spirit art', hoping to leave it at that. This of course started the very inquisitive lecturers talking and wanting to know what my work entailed, never having heard about it. I tried to deflect the question with another question about their artwork but at this particular time I was not able not do that. I explained that this type of artwork is quite rare and the first known artists are documented to have come from western New York State in the 1840's, and only a few people create art in this way. I went on to say that, "I obtain impressions from the spirit world which I then draw or paint" which seemed to give more fuel to the lecturers inquisitiveness and, unfortunately, created a deluge of other questions. One young lecturer sitting next to me whose art work was beautifully coloured felting said; "I don't like the idea of that" and continued to tell us that she had a psychic drawing from a woman who was a medium when her sister took her to a spiritualist church and, staring straight ahead, eyes becoming wide perhaps with fear remembering the event, she said she was petrified to go back. "I am a Born Again Christian now" she said "and what the woman did un-nerved all of us. She drew a portrait of my sister who died of cancer five years ago and I believe we should not call upon the dead."

Obviously I was in attendance at the meeting as an art lecturer not a medium but I asked her to explain what happened at the church. Apparently, during a demonstration of psychic art, the medium, a young woman, pointed to her and said she had a woman in spirit who had died of cancer and she had drawn a picture of her. The medium then turned the paper around and she had drawn her sister. Unfortunately during the event the lecturer was so shocked she felt ill and had to leave the church. She said she got no comfort out of the demonstration and had not asked for her sister to come to her for any reason. At this point our lecturers meeting resumed and the receiver of the picture was left up in the air pale with the shock of recounting the experience. I was not able to help or discuss the situation with her because she left the meeting early. I am saddened that the lecturer's sister was not able to get her message across because all the sister may have wanted to say at that time was; 'I am OK now... I CAN go on to the place where I need to be' and be able to leave the earthiness of the physical world, but for some unknown reason this young woman was not able to cope with any message from the dead.

I have never experienced a negative situation at any of my demonstrations or readings like this but I am sure that whoever the spirit artist was she would have liked to have given the appropriate message to the right person, and maybe that is why I was sitting next to her at the lecturers' meeting that day, perhaps to help her sister to complete her journey and I hope she is able to eventually leave her message and she is able to move on.

Chapter Six

SPIRIT PORTRAITS AND CASE STUDIES

I have so many stories to tell, about the portraits I have painted and sketches drawn in many countries of the world and for so many different people, that I wasn't sure where to start. I have drawn thousands of portraits since the early 1980's most of them at public demonstrations which have been given away. I think this aspect of 'give away' is something unique to spirit artists because if I put my artist hat on and I am commissioned to paint pictures which I then sell, I make an income because that is my job, but with spirit art all the artwork in demonstrations is given away to the recipient because the portrait cannot belong to anyone else and, more importantly, the message from spirit is in the portrait.

For this section entitled Case Studies, I have chosen some very significant and life changing examples of what I do and where I do it. I will be writing about a few of the portraits which seem to have made a difference to the person who has received them and also to the person in spirit. In public demonstrations I have approximately an hour to produce as many portraits as I can for the people who have come to see me draw them, and, in that time I draw between 5 and 6 portraits depending on the spiritual understanding of the recipient. Sometimes people have never met their ancestors or the people in spirit who I draw, sometimes they have been adopted and their real parents come through. When I start I never know who is going to be drawn, this is not my choice. In the world of spirit my guides and those who are going to be drawn get ready for their fleeting moment to give their message.

I have often been asked how it works from the spirit side of life. OK, I will try to explain, although sometimes the words are not adequate enough to explain what actually happens.

To begin with, I am the artist drawing the portraits in the physical world, however, without contact with the spirit world I would be making the drawings up, they would not be spirit drawings, and that would be cheating and immoral! Sometimes my spirit art students say they think they are imagining the portrait when they first start because they are working in the 'dark' clairsentiently, however once the verbal message they have received from spirit and the drawing which has been drawn with the aid of spirit go together and both are recognised they are soon impressed with what they have been able to achieve, and they will go on to do more.

Spirit Portraiture: Loved Ones

Below I have written about some of the many spirit portraits I have drawn which have been witnessed and recognised by the receivers of the drawings. These case studies not only show how diverse the portraits can be but also how far they travel and to whom. There have been several artist guides working through me as my control and I have tried to explain the techniques and methods I have used for each case study explaining how each portrait was created.

1987: The man with the moustache

I was just beginning my spiritual journey with my new interest in spirit art and I was asked by my friend and medium Tommy Richardson to join him for a demonstration of mediumship at Wrexham Spiritualist Church. I accepted and once I had finished work at school I collected Tommy from the Psychic Truth Centre where he lived and began the two hour journey to

Wrexham. I had not served the church before but Tommy was a well liked medium and had Spiritualist services all over the North West of England. I was unsure as to how long the drive would take and at that time there was no such thing as a Sat. Nav. so I dashed home, quickly changed, picked up my art equipment and drove to where Tommy lived.

We liked to arrive at our venue about half an hour to spare so as to rest and make the important links with the spirit world, but the traffic and weather was so poor that we just made it to the small red brick church with a few moments to spare. I quickly set-up my art equipment as the service was about to start. Tommy began with the prayers of invocation and a short explanation of what we were to do that evening. We had agreed that he would be giving individual messages from the spirit world while I was drawing and then I would give my message together with the portrait.

The evening began as it usually did with Tommy, a very humorous man, reducing the congregation to tears with laughter so when it was my time to give my message and find the owner of the spirit portrait it took a while for them to calm down. Eventually my words could be heard. I had written information which had come to me clairaudiently at the side of the conte drawn image so when it was my turn I was able to give the information before showing the drawing. I asked if there was a lady in the congregation who had lower area back pain who could link with a gentleman whose name I felt was James. The character of the man was excitable and he would have suffered with a nervous stomach. He wore glasses but lost the sight in one eye before passing and with this man I was given information regarding mining connections.

A lady, towards the right of the room, put her hand up and said that the description and information sounded like her grandfather. I asked if he had a moustache which I had drawn on the paper, she quite adamantly said no. There was no-one else in the room who could accept the information and the lady said that the drawing looked like her grandfather (without the moustache) so I gave her the picture.

It was over six months later when I revisited the Church again, without Tommy this time, for a special demonstration of Spirit Art and the lady who received the drawing was present. She came to me after the service because she had a photograph with the original drawing in her hand and said she had gone through all the photographs of James and on one of them he indeed had a moustache. The photograph was taken at a time she would not have known him and so would not have seen the moustache. She kindly said I could keep the picture for my records which I was very pleased to do. It was proof that sometimes when the recipient says no it may mean, maybe, because sometimes they would not know until they have a look, as this lady did, through the photographs.

Of the many thousands of drawings I have drawn world-wide, and which have been recognised, I have very few to show for the work I have done. Indeed, a lady in Wolverhampton was given a drawing at a church service in 1992 and in 2005 she was able to show me a photograph of the gentleman, who turned out to be her great grandfather who she had never met. She had just received a box of photographs because a member of the family had died and she inherited the photograph albums. She put the spirit drawing together with one of the photographs and the match was conclusive. Until then she didn't know who the portrait was of. When a portrait is given to someone who does not recognise the person I no longer worry about the conclusiveness of image because I am now aware that whatever is drawn is important and sometimes it is not the spirit world who make the mistake in recognising the portrait or the evidence to go with it… it is the person who receives the portrait, who may never have met or known about the person. The drawings are all important no matter whom they are for or what they are about, sometimes it can take many years to identify the drawing and give credence to the information.

1987: Frank

Drawings and paintings come to people in many different ways and the next example is a very strange one indeed. In 1986 I was invited to a Women's Institute in Warrington to demonstrate mediumship for a charity event. I often work for charity events helping to bring some money into the coffers for them. However, the downside is many of the people who come are just looking for entertainment and are very shocked by the outcome of some of the accurate messages.

It was quite a warm early spring evening and the ladies had apparently had a 'bring and buy' during the day and were finishing the day off with a 'show'. The venue was a typical small wooden village hall outside Warrington with quite a large stage for me to do my work. There were half length windows to the right as I stood on the stage and a folding wall to the left where the women volunteers were finishing off clearing the tea cups away. The hall quickly and efficiently filled up and I was introduced as an evening of something different. I was not demonstrating spirit art that evening, only mediumship; however I did have a card up my sleeve for the final curtain. I knew that an audience who came to these events from outside an understanding of Spiritualism were sometimes difficult because some are unwilling to speak up in front of those they know, about the people who have died. They think of it as entertainment, which is not my view at all, but it takes all types of meetings to spread the understanding of the spirit world.

I began by speaking about myself and what I did for a living. Being a school teacher in Toxteth Liverpool could have been an evening talk on its own but within a few moments I had the audience laughing with a few anecdotes of my life as a schoolmarm in Liverpool.

Soon after the initial warming up I explained what my role was in the evening's event but also their role. If they have any connection with any information I should give out to the audience they should speak up. I explained how I had not received a message myself because I was shy and I would not like that to happen to them, after all, the spirit world may only have this one window to put their message across. The evening was slow at first but soon the ladies were accepting the information and the evening was beginning to take off.

At about 20 minutes before the end I was called to time but I had one more message to give. I explained that I was able to draw portrait of someone in spirit without being in the hall with the receivers of the messages. I can draw the picture at home and complete the message in the venue. I also told them I was a spirit artist and I could draw the people who were going to be present before I arrived and that I had drawn a portrait a few days earlier at home by linking into the future energy which would be present in the hall

77

that evening. At that point there was a little chatter of puzzlement. I went to the edge of the stage and collected a drawing.

A few days earlier I had sat at my easel and quickly drawn a portrait of a man and written a few bits of information at the top of the picture. I was told clairaudiently that his name was Frank and he passed very suddenly of a heart attack. He had something to do with the forces and he would have worked on engines because I could smell the engine oil and see his hands and fingernails which were oily and greasy. I took the drawing to the demonstration that night and began to read the information. Everybody in the room was cheery until I began to read the details and the ambient sound became hushed. I asked again if there was anyone who would like to take the drawing. It was as though I had said John F Kennedy had died! The host rushed onto the stage and broke the silence by saying what a wonderful evening they had had and how much money they had raised.

The curtains were closed and the chair of the Women's Institute came close to me like a figure out of a Margaret Rutherford film. She took my elbow and moved me into the shadows of the curtains. 'Yes' she said, 'that is Frank but, unfortunately, both his wife <u>and</u> lover were in the audience tonight and neither would speak out. What an embarrassing moment for all involved!' She took the drawing and said she would do what she could for me. A few weeks later I received an envelope with a photocopy of the drawing and a small passport photo, nothing else, but at least Frank could now rest in peace since he had made his presence felt in the Halls of the Women's Institute!

2009: Hollie

I had helped Walsall Spiritualist Church in the West Midlands many times to create an income to support the upkeep of the church and the 13th June 2009 was no exception. The Church President Jo Blackmore phoned me several weeks before the demonstration to ascertain if the date was still all right for me to do it. Yes it was and it looked as though it was going to be another wonderful evening. A few months before I had produced six drawings for the congregation which included one for the Mayor of Walsall who, between herself her husband and driver they received three lovely portraits ranging from the mayor's school friend to her husband's father to a wonderful gentleman who came through to speak to their chauffeur wearing an Indian police turban, giving advice on driving in crowded conditions.

However, the weather conditions were not so good this particular evening and there were less than forty people attending the evening of mediumship. As usual I began talking a little about myself and what I was going to do during the evening. I had a large flip chart to work on which meant that I was able to work 'automatically' with my artist guides. I had already produced two or three drawings and then began to draw a pastel sketch of a young girl. I remember saying the names, Dolly, Molly, Polly and then Holly, and from the front of the church, just a few rows to the left in front of me, I heard a gasp and a lady said that is Hollie, my grand-daughter. She passed with Leukaemia but the clairsentience I had given out to the audience, as part of the message, was one of a temperature but with a pain to the front temples, I said that it was a pain in my head similar to a childhood illness. The grandmother was so excited that Hollie had been drawn she took out her mobile phone and showed me a photograph taken of Hollie as a bridesmaid. I had drawn her with butterflies in her hair and on the photograph she had her hair up with the butterflies in it. The grandmother said that she would show it to her daughter, Hollie's mother, and email me with the response.

That September the pastel picture of Hollie was proudly exhibited at The Ancient High House in Stafford for the second Spirit Art Society exhibition of psychic and spirit art. Wendy had given me the original artwork and her granddaughter was exhibited at the Gallery together with evidential photographs and the information regarding the demonstration which was a few weeks earlier. At the opening of the exhibition Wendy spoke about how Hollie had a favourite book called The Brave Little Train which she used to read to her and how Hollie's cousin, Bethany, tells Wendy that Hollie is well! Wendy knows this because of things Bethany says to her about Hollie. For example, Bethany was too young to know what Hollie's favourite book was, yet Bethany told Wendy that Hollie's favourite book was *The Brave Little Train* and that she often came to see her and play.

Wendy was pleased to allow me to retain the original portrait so I had a poster size copy made up for her which was sent to Hollie's mother to frame and put in her room. The Spirit Art Society retains the original and will exhibit the story at each exhibition while travelling to show the work done by spirit artists. To me this is a unique story about how the spirit world gives us evidence every single day to help the spirit world say…'Hello…we are here again….and we try to come to you in so many different ways.'

2007: Mother-in-law appears in Halfpenny Green Winery

As part of my work as a sprit artist I am asked to teach classes or workshops to other mediums or prospective mediums or spirit artists and in 2007 I was asked to teach a day workshop for Gill who had a crystal shop in the middle of a vineyard in the middle of England. The shop was like an Aladdin's cave with a small room to the back where the workshop was being held. It was a hot summer's day and the room was very stuffy. I had already taught for a few hours and the sun had gone off the side windows so I opened the curtains which had been shielding us from the heat and light and opened the window. As I did so, I saw an elderly lady up on the top of a hill in front of the bungalow behind the vineyard. I remarked to the group that there was a lady up on the hill and started to describe her. She was absolutely solid and did not look like a spirit at all. She was looking towards us and as I turned away and back she had disappeared. I thought she had gone into the house. There was an audible gasp from the back of the room and one of the students said 'are you sure she is really there?' I said, "No! But I will draw the lady now and describe her personality." Which I did!

As I was drawing and explaining the character of the lady I noticed the student had put her hands to her face in shock so I asked if she was alright. She said that she wasn't and would explain once I had finished. The drawing, in pastel, was one of an elderly lady with a stern face and piercing blue eyes. She wore a blue cardigan and her hair was silver, thick on the top and short at the sides and back. She was a formidable looking lady with a character to match. Once I had completed the verbal information, plus the drawing, I asked the student who she thought the lady was. She said that she had never been to anything like this before and she was not a medium but very interested in it and the drawing was an exact likeness of her mother-in-law who used to live in the bungalow and was the owner of the vineyard. She couldn't wait to show the portrait to her husband and when asked if the original could be exhibited at the first Spirit Art Exhibition she said it could. Her husband did not previously believe in life after death (nor did his mother) and couldn't understand how I could draw her so accurately without knowing her, but thought it was an excellent image of her.

I have said before that I have done thousands of these drawings but so few are given back to me to keep. It is wonderful to be able to sketch the pictorial information showing that a person can be drawn after death as evidence of life after mortal death, it is only now that I can take digital photographs of both the drawing and the evidence to keep for myself and keep a record of what I can do with the help of spirit. This is particularly helpful when I am working in other countries and the example below is proof of that.

2007: German Grandfather

I have had the honour of visiting Germany twice and while I am there I am hosted by a wonderful young woman who has a PhD in Languages and is a medium herself. As I create the drawings and give the message she will translate from the English into German and vice versa. On my second visit I was asked to demonstrate Spirit Art in a small leisure and health centre in a small town near Frankfurt. Again the weather was not too good and just a handful of people arrived and it was lovely to be able to give either a drawing or a message to all of the attendees with the help of my host who translated my English into German while I was giving the message.

I had already given three or four messages with drawings when I began to draw on flip chart paper, in brown pastel, the face of a man with a huge white moustache wearing a felted green warm winter coat. I gave the lady some names and places, not so much in German but mostly in Austrian. The lady said at the time she was not sure if this was her grandfather because she had never met him but she would find out and send me a picture by email.

Several months later I received an email from her with a photograph attached. She apologised for not being able to help at the time because she couldn't find a picture of him but had now emailed the small portrait from her grandfather's passport which was Austrian. There were a few things I said about him which she had never known but it was her mother who filled in the information and was so pleased to have a portrait of him. The mother had been thinking about him for a couple of days previous to my drawing the portrait and said that it was an excellent likeness.

2007: American college lecturer is drawn for New Yorker

The year I travelled to Germany I also visited New York as the guest of a very fine medium who I had met in the Arthur Findlay College while undergoing training as a tutor. I was very interested in seeing the precipitated paintings of the Bangs Sisters at the Lily Dale Assembly, western New York State, where Dr Lauren Thibodaux had a summer house. Lauren's house was opposite Lizzie and May's house where they lived while working at Lily Dale in the late nineteenth and early twentieth century which was very fortuitous for me. Also, at the top of Library Road, was the Lily Dale Museum where many of the rare paintings are exhibited. There are strict rules against visiting or outside mediums working while they are visiting the Assembly so I watched how American mediums worked in the Assembly room where all the regular mediums met each day.

I could not practice my drawing in Lily Dale but while I was in New York I was introduced to a lovely young lady who was an artist and very interested in what I did, so, very spontaneously, as though the spirit world had been waiting a long time to reach her, I started a drawing. It soon became clear to her that the drawing was of a gentleman who was her art lecturer at College who was also interested in the theatre. Obviously I had never met the lady before and knew nothing about her, but the art lecturer in spirit began talking about the theatre and painting stage sets and working on costumes as though he knew a great deal about what she did for a living. After a few very quiet moments the lady admitted that she worked on Broadway and the gentleman was her Art Lecturer from College who worked in the theatre while he was alive. She was surprised to receive a drawing of him and not her father who had just passed to spirit. Her father had spoken through me to her in the reading but his was not the portrait to be drawn.

This is a question most people ask; "Why is one person drawn and not another and why is the one person who is thought of the most not drawn?" To my knowledge the person who is drawn is the one who the person needs the most in life at that particular time. For example; if I am decorating my house I would not need help from my housewife Auntie who never worked, it would be my Uncle whose job it was to paint and decorate. The Auntie may be interested in the colour scheme but not the practicalities of decorating. If I was moving house my own father may come close to help me because this is what he did for a living, he was a removals manager and helped people relocate.

So back to the drawing I did in New York, why was it her lecturer and not her father? Well at that time she was working in the theatre and just looking for a new position. The reading detailed things she could do, from her lecturer, who would have had experience of such matters, to help her. He father spoke to her and gave her that sort of comfort; however, the Lecturer gave her insight into opportunities in her life which her father would have wanted too but not had experience of in his lifetime.

On one visit to Belfast a lady came to see me for a drawing and because it was not who she desperately wanted I drew another for her. The second was not who she wanted either but the verbal reading came from the two sons she had lost to spirit very recently by taking their own life. She also asked why they were not drawn and the only answer I could give was that the other two people wanted to help her over the suicides of both her boys, who had come back to say sorry to her and to prove she had support around her. The boys had been through to her several times and were waiting in the wings in this reading. I am afraid the answer was of no help to the lady and I hope that at some time she will be able to understand that we cannot demand what we want from the spirit world. They try their best to help as far as possible.

2009: Margaret, the nun, is drawn for niece in Belfast

During a second visit to Belfast I was asked to demonstrate spirit art in a leisure centre in Hollywood. At the end of the meeting I thought I had completed all the drawings, however, and just as I put my pastels down, I heard from my guide in spirit, 'There's another one to be done.' I had been called to time by the Chairperson and was not expecting another drawing. Very quickly I drew the portrait of a very thin faced woman with grey straight hair, almost dishevelled. It was only as I completed the rather austere woman I realised she was wearing a nun's habit. Her name was Margaret and she wanted to speak to her niece who she looked after as a child. The niece spoke out to say that the drawing was exactly as Margaret was just before she died in the convent where she last saw her. Margaret's character was rather brusque as she asked me to tell her niece that all those arguments they had had over religion she realises now that her niece was right...that her spirit has continued after death and she just wanted to come back and say that. As a nun in the Catholic Church while she was alive, she could not accept the reasoning that all souls go to the spirit world, but of course now she does. It was also poignant that as a nun she would not have a photograph taken of her and the niece had no record of her but she would allow the portrait to be drawn to prove she was there. Her niece admitted that they did have many disagreements over where the soul went and she was glad Sister Margaret had come to see her on that day, the niece's birthday.

2010: Portraits to Dubai

In the autumn of 2009 I was contacted, by email, by a lady who I had never met and who lives out in Dubai. She said that she had come across my web site on the internet and she would like to commission a painting. She said that she wasn't sure which type to have and would leave it up to me. Because of my worsening health due to my regular visits to the hospital for venesection, to relieve the problems caused by Hereditary Haemachromotosis, I delayed the portraits as long as until nearly a month before Christmas, but felt they needed to be away soon in case of any Christmas postal backlog. She specified one portrait but I felt I needed to draw one and paint another. Sometimes the spirit world has an agenda which we mere mortals do not know about until after an event has happened.

I painted a soul portrait for her in watercolours on watercolour paper which was absolutely beautiful and felt, while I was painting, that she was a very special soul. The second was of an American Indian who gave a lot of evidence regarding his life, what sort of place he lived in and began telling his story. As I was painting I was talking into a Dictaphone ready to transfer onto a compact disc and as I completed the two portraits I suddenly felt the urge to draw another portrait.

This time I did not tell her because I felt the spirit world wanted the third to be a gift from spirit. The drawing and dictated reading began and I realised it was a school age boy I was drawing. Much of the reading I don't remember now, and, anyway it was very personal to the recipient. I completed the very light and bright drawing and started to pack the portraits away to mail to her so she would receive the drawings especially for Christmas.

I was told by the post office staff that the portraits should only take a week to fly to Dubai so I thought they would be there quickly. After returning from post office I emailed the lady and told her what they had said and that she should receive them within the week. Well, the portraits took three weeks to get to Dubai but she received them before Christmas. She emailed me a day after she had received them and said that when she saw them they reduced her to tears, not because they were bad, but because they were beautiful and so full of meaning. The boy was a lost child known to her and the Indian guide was Yellow Wolf who had been with her for a long time. She said that as I gave the reading she could 'see' the Indian village, smell the wood burning and feel the slight chill in the air. I was unaware that she was a Spiritualist medium and teacher and I was so pleased to eventually meet up with her the following February. And, as I had felt in the reading she is such a beautiful soul.

Spirit Portraiture: Guardian Angels

2007: Angelic Presence, New York

Occasionally I will receive an order for a portrait by email and usually the order is from overseas. The next case study is about a portrait which was commissioned by one person but meant for another. In the spring of 2006 I was contacted by a healer who worked in New York. Diane was a lady I had never met and knew nothing about her or even where she lived, because the address to send the portrait to was a box number. There have been occasions when an order has come from someone who has never met the actual buyer so there is no opportunity for collusion. However, this particular order I was able to do straight away, I felt well, good in myself and was ready and willing to have a go, but each time I sat down to draw the portrait I did not feel impressed to do anything for the lady. I tried several times over several weeks, and yet there was no inspiration. I was puzzled until I sat down and instead of asking for a drawing for the lady I asked my guide for a drawing which has to be done for whatever reason and sent to this lady.

I set to and was inspired to paint, firstly, one portrait that looked like a policeman and then I was inspired to draw another portrait of an angelic young girl. She had only asked for one portrait but, if I am inspired to draw more than one drawing that's what I have to do. I usually record my voice as I am painting. I do seem to be talking to myself but I am actually speaking directly to the person about the portraits. The first portrait of the New York policeman was drawn very quickly as though he had been waiting for a while to be noticed, and in view of the wait I had before drawing him, I am not surprised. He gave his evidence about what happened to him during the Twin Towers collapse on 9/11, some names and that he was just about to retire.

Diane's apartment, she later told me, was within view of the collapse of the towers so she was not surprised her friend had come through to speak to her. I then realised why I couldn't start my drawings for her because there was a second to be done and her husband had to go through an experience before I drew the portrait.

The second turned out to be a portrait of a very beautiful young girl about the age of six. She had long blonde hair and very bright blue-green eyes which sparkled when she smiled. I completed a watercolour portrait of her and parcelled them both off and sent them to New York. A while later I had an email from Dianne. She said she had received the portraits and the one of the girl was, at first rather puzzling, and later, enlightenment for her husband. You see, what had happened was her husband a week or so earlier was awoken from his sleep in the middle of the night to see a child's figure floating over the top of Dianne's body. Dianne was sound asleep and the figure frightened him so he didn't speak of it. When the drawing arrived she opened it and could not understand why she had received it. Only when her husband came home and asked why there was a drawing of the girl on the dining room table did it all make sense. He then admitted to seeing the girl in his half sleep state and didn't want to say anything until the reading fitted into place.

He had been married before and his ex wife had lost a baby who they knew to be a girl. His other children were ash blonde in hair colour and so the spirit girl fitted him, but why had she come, he asked? I hadn't known this but he was suffering from post traumatic stress disorder having witnessed the towers going down and I believe his spirit daughter was there to help him through it. He was having nightmares about hundreds of people dying all at once and couldn't comprehend what may have happened to them before and after death. Receiving a portrait of his daughter brought to him the realisation that there was, after all, an afterlife which eased his inner pain. Why the girl was floating over Dianne we are not sure but the message was given to him and he understood why.

2007: John sketched for his sister

Although I am now retired from teaching in schools and colleges I still do a little examining and moderating work so I don't have too much time to sit for a private reading with people. However, some people call me on the phone and if I can do a drawing for the person I will try. Because of my hospital treatments I sometimes make the appointment and then can be too poorly to do it, but this one particular occasion everything was right with the world and a reading for a boy's sister fell into place.

I had met John's sister while doing a demonstration of spirit art at Wolverhampton Spiritualist Church and she asked if I did private readings. I said I don't do many but if she phoned me I would see if I could find a time to see her. She duly phoned and we set a date. I didn't know what she wanted she seemed a nice person and genuine so I was happy to do this for her. The week before she came I was very poorly after having hospital treatment and wondered if I should cancel. I phoned her mobile number a few times but it seemed she had changed her number so my message wasn't going through to her. I hoped she would phone me but on the day she was due to arrive I felt a little better and as the time drew near for her reading I was back to normal. She arrived and I took her into my garage studio where I do my artwork. We sat down and I explained that I had no control over whom I draw and that I could not even guarantee a drawing. She said she understood that and she knew I would do my best.

As I began drawing I suddenly began to cough and sensed a strong young man overshadowing me. I asked him, in my mind, to move away a little and I continued with my drawing, he was very obliging and seemed to have a rather boyish personality. From the spirit world he was making comments about my drawing as though he wanted to have a go too. As I spoke about the information he was giving to me the young lady broke down in tears and said that she had hoped and prayed he would come to her. It was so important to her that he came through that tears began to fall from my eyes from him. He said he was sorry for what he did and why he had to take his own life, but he couldn't see another way out. She understood everything and when I turned the portrait around she said "that's just like him" and produced some photographs she had in her pocket to prove it. From her pocket and mobile she produced several photographs and on one of them he was shown with a spirit orb above his head. I said there was a spirit baby in the orb to which the lady said she understood that especially at the time the photo was taken.

John had taken his own life because he didn't know which way to turn when he got into trouble. His sister needed to know why he had done it and he told her in the verbal messages and the drawing. He could now rest in peace. He said he would never forget her and once he had adjusted to the spirit world he would always come to her when she thought about him. John's portrait is the reason why I do this work. The family were desperate to know he was all right and he knew, once he had passed to spirit, what a mistake he had made and that there were many loving people around him who could have helped. I wonder if John's story may help others try to find help rather than take their own life?

After finishing the portrait and after John's sister left me I began to feel awful again and went straight to bed. The spirit world had given me a short porthole of health and spirit light in order to do the work and each time I see his sister and family at Wolverhampton Church they thank me so much, but I always tell them it is not me, I cannot do this work without the aid of the spirit world, it is those who love the family, our guides and our teachers who instigate and bring people together.

Spirit Portraits: Spirit Guides And Teachers

We all have spirit guides or guardian angels helping us in our earth existence and whether we know they are there or not, or who they are, it actually does not matter, because they would still do the job they have chosen to do from the spirit world, whether we like it or not! Some medium's see our guides as angelic forces, others as just ordinary people giving us a helping hand, whichever way you think about them they are all doing the same work and that is; firstly, not to interfere in our destiny and secondly, to help us when we are in need. I usually don't know who is guiding me in my daily life, but I do know they are there to help me and whether it is Great Aunt Daisy or the Reverend Carter, I don't try to find out, it doesn't matter. When I am drawing the spirit portraits I **know** my guides are there because I can feel that there are different personalities standing with me, and as artists they all have their own style and presence. I don't need to find out exactly who they are because they are working fine with me and I wouldn't like to spoil that.

I do know that when I am baking a cake Aunt Rene, who was a great cook, comes in to help, and when drawing a portrait (not a spirit portrait but my own work) one of my artist Great Aunt's will come in to help. When I am driving to a church, at a time before Sat. Nav's, my RAC or AA guide will come in (no I am joking!), a friend who used to drive for a living will come in to help me get to the church on time. So, each spirit guide will help in the way they know best. I wouldn't look through the yellow pages for a bricklayer when I am in need of a painter and decorator, so when we are in need in our earthly existence we will be helped by our family guides, our spiritual guides or the angels, depending on which job needs to be done.

Our spirit guides have a different role to our more practical guides and exist in a slightly different place in the world of spirit. As a spirit artist and healer I have different guides for both spiritual aspects; a set of guides specifically for healing, and, a set of artists or teachers for the art, and of course when I am writing I will have another who will help me write (and believe me I need a good guide for the writing!). I say a 'set of guides' because those developing spiritual abilities will have more than one subject-orientated guide as we develop into the area of spirit work we do. For example as we are learning the fundamentals of healing or meditation we may have a spirit school-teacher, then as we get better our guiding force steps up a notch and the teacher becomes a lecturer and as we develop further the lecturer will become a Master, and this system will follow through until we are a master at what we are doing ourselves. My spirit guides are different even within the disciplines. If I paint in Acrylics I will have an artist who would have worked in acrylics in his mortal life, if I am Earth healing, rather than human body healing, I will have a guide who understands the properties of earth healing. And so will you.

Then we have guardian angels, which is a book in itself and I am sure there are many books written on the subject so I won't go too deeply into them here, but these guides will be with us for specific reasons in our lives and perhaps only once. Many years ago when I was a school teacher I had left school and was on my way to visit a friend who lived about an hour away. I drove through the Liverpool tunnel and onto the motorway through the other side. I knew where I was going, the traffic was light and it was a beautiful summer evening. I was about two miles from the roundabout at the junction I needed in order to get to my friend's house. I tried to speed up and put my foot on the accelerator (I am a slow driver at the best of times) but realised the car was slowing down. My foot had pushed the accelerator right down onto the floor but I was still slowing down and wondered if there was something wrong with the car? Then, just before I reached the roundabout at the end of the motorway, a van with several men in it overtook me at speed. It was as though the world went into slow motion; the men in the van were drinking from cans of lager and one had thrown a can out of the van as he passed me. As they reached the roundabout I was slightly behind them, they did not slow up and the van caught the curb and turned right over. The reason why I am writing about this event is because if my car had not [been] slowed up I would be dead or seriously injured under their van. I believe that an angelic force slowed my car down so I would not be dead. I have had three events in my life when I have been saved from severe accidents but I feel that this one is the most profound and life saving. I did not sense anything or see anything or anybody with wings and I realised afterwards that if I had not been slowed down I would be writing this from spirit!

In the First World War many of the troops going 'over the top' later spoke about how they could hear the whistle of the bullets pass their ears as they were running, seeing their comrades go down, but they were not hit, wounded nor killed. They used to have the phrase that the bullet 'did not have their name on it'. They, for some reason were helped by the angelic realms to survive the war, perhaps, only to go on to save someone else.

As a spirit artist I have been able to draw many of these guiding lights in the spirit world. I have drawn, painted and sketched many a mediums working guide or healer's spiritual guide and although there is little evidence that these guides actually exist. Many sensitives feel a change in energy with them when they are working, and so, believe there to be someone else working with them. Below I am going to give a few examples of the types of guides who are working with people and why. When creating a drawing of a guide I work at a different vibrational frequency than when I am drawing evidential portraits, because I am usually working in a semi trance state when drawing automatically with a spirit artist guiding the strokes. I will explain how I am producing these automatic drawings as I go along.

2010: An unexpected visitor helps at a Workshop

During an art workshop in the Ancient High House in Stafford there were some very lovely people attending. Some of them I had taught before and some I had never met before. I explain to them that the spirit world would have arranged each student to have a teaching guide or artist with them during the workshop to help them draw from the spirit world. As the students were working on their first task I began to automatically draw the guide who would be working with me for the day. When I draw automatically I allow a spirit artist to draw through me using my own abilities as an artist to make their drawing. The style of drawing and mark making methods utilised by the guide usually gives me an idea of who the guide is.

On that particular day my hand was swiftly taken over and a drawing was produced in pastel chalks on the white paper hung on the flip chart. We were all surprised at the portrait which evolved on the paper because he looked like a well-known artist. Suddenly we realised that he looked like the Flemish artist, Anthony van Dyke (1599-1641). Fortunately we were in a historic building and we asked if the manager could come to speak to us about the drawing. She said the drawing was very interesting because van Dyke was the portrait painter to King Charles I and he had stayed in the house several times. The portrait painter Anthony van Dyke was one of the major artists who painted him. We all laughed because of the news that such a famous artist as van Dyke had deemed it important to visit us and guide us that day! A lovely portrait was automatically drawn for us and a piece of historic knowledge to go with it! I don't really go with the idea of famous artist's as guides, but that day I seemed to be shown a different viewpoint.

1993: American Indian guide comes to visit

I have many stories like the ones I have just recounted, but one of the most surprising and rewarding for me was when my daughter was very little and we had just moved to Stafford. I had just woken from the night's sleep and saw a figure of an American Indian in full chief's costume standing at the bottom of the bed as solid as I am. I was rather surprised but not as frightened as I was the night my nun guide arrived just before my father's death! My husband was asleep and, as I looked into the soulful brown eyes of the chief I heard him say, 'I know you will do a good job for my friend.' Baffled, I said thank you, to the large strong man. As he faded away I heard the post-box bang in the hallway downstairs just as our mail came through the letter box. My daughter had heard it too and with her small young legs jumped downstairs to pick them up. As she was coming back up stairs, obviously checking the mail for us, she said; 'Mummy, there is a funny looking letter here.' And, as she brought it to me, I realised it was an airmail letter from Australia from the look of the large kangaroo stamp in the corner of the envelope.

I wondered who the letter was from since I didn't know anyone over in Australia at the time. I took out a neatly folded piece of thin blue airmail paper which was a note to say that the lady who sent the letter had been in England visiting family and she had seen one of my paintings at a family member's house. She said that she had always wanted a painting of her healing guide who had been with her since she was very young. As I read the letter I was humbled by what she said in the note. She had always known that she had a guide or guiding angel with her from birth who has always helped her in life and gave healing to others when they were sick. The painting she required was of an American Indian Chief who stands at the bottom of her bed every morning when she awakes!

I painted the portrait of the Chief who had visited me that day and posted it off to her with a note telling her he had also visited me the same morning. What wonderful proof that the spirit world can move through time and space as easily as blinking. The lady wrote again to say how good the likeness was of her guide and to thank me for doing it so quickly. I really had no choice. When the spirit world want something doing now it has to be done. When I say this I am also saying that sometimes they wait for months before completing the request for guides and loved ones. I have come to realise that if there is a wait then the person either may not be ready for the guide or they have to go through something in their life before they receive the drawing. As I have said before I have no choice, if I begin a drawing without their assistance the drawing will be wrong. I have to wait for the inspiration from the other world to get the portrait completed right. I remember one lady, who did not understand this concept, and, since she was also rather annoyed she said she didn't want the portrait, a few months later she gave up on her work as a Spiritualist.

2005 A guiding light in my meditation

I try to meditate at least once a day, but sometimes the hustle and bustle of life takes over and I can't. I can't remember the exact month now, it was sometime in early Spring 2005 when I found I had a chance to meditate in my art studio. I had a piece of music playing and began to drift off into the swirls of colour I assume to be the first lights of the energy in the spirit world. My meditations are transcendental and I began to lose awareness of my physical body as the colours around me became lighter in shade and sensation.

Suddenly a familiar face began to emerge out of the spiritual light, a face from the past visiting me for a reason. The man came nearer and as he did so I heard, clairsentiently, within my head, 'I have come to ask you to paint my portrait for the church, will you be able to do that for me, my dear?' The face and the voice were that of Gordon Higginson the President of the Spiritualist National Union and past President of Longton Spiritualist Church who had passed into spirit many years previously. Gordon was such a famous medium, and close to the heart of many a Spiritualist, I so I felt awkward creating a portrait of him in his enlightened colours but I had said I would do it and I did, twice!

I created the first portrait and offered it to the then president of Longton Church. Unfortunately there was a dispute in the church and the President took it home, where it stayed. Many years later I heard Gordon say that the painting should be in the church but I could not retrieve it so I changed the image and copied it onto canvas three times. The copies were then over-painted in acrylic showing the lights which were around Gordon at that time in spirit and the paintings all have a different energy to them. Longton Church was given one of the paintings and I kept my promise to Gordon. I have one copy on my studio wall and a very special friend has another. Gordon loved the church which he and his mother Fanny looked after while on the earth and I felt that his energy would help the church in many ways.

Soul Portraits

Many people starting out in Spiritualism ask me the difference between our soul and our spirit. Well, the way I understand the concept to be, the spirit is the core of us and is eternal, the soul is an amalgamation of lives, experiences and knowledge, and as we develop spiritually certain parts of our soul dissipate into the ether revealing more of our core spirit. I have tried to analyse this highly discussed concept and break it down into simpler blocks of information. Firstly, while we are alive our spirit is part of us but is able to move through time and space which is similar to when we are in the afterlife itself. Our spirit is the accumulation of our 'unconditional love' and spiritual energy. You may say, well, what is our soul then? Is it our spirit or our mind? The word soul has connotations with Christianity and other religions; however, it does help us understand our role as a spirit. I will try to describe what the spirit is without going too deeply into the philosophy and, if you have other ideas, then that's good too.

As a physical entity living in a physical world we are made up of a spirit, a soul and physical body. We know what our physical body is and that it lives for a certain time then dies. The spirit is the energy we all have which is in existence before life, during, and after the physical body dies and is said to be an eternal energy. The soul is made up of several parts or etheric bodies, and these parts include the souls of past life energies and any other forms we have taken in our total existence. Now, this is a difficult concept to understand and for thousands of years philosophers have discussed just this point, so if you have a different point of view to me then your opinion may follow Siedenburg or Socrates or any one of our previous masters, and maybe, we will need to be in existence in our etheric body before we fully and truly understand what each and every part is.

Developing my point further, the core spirit has what I call several 'bolt-on's' which are the previous lives we have had in order to gain the experiences we need to reach our destiny in our physical life, and these, when put together, may be called our 'soul'. The soul contains all the knowledge we have acquired both in and out of our physical body and is part of our spirit and yet separate from it as well. An onion is made is of skin, layers and a centre [core]. If we can think of our physical body like the skin of an onion and when we die we take the skin [the physical body] off and are left with the same size and shape which has many layers [the soul]. As we peel further we come to the centre core which is analogous to the spirit, take the core to nothing and we have infinity. So, when we pass to spirit at death, the shape and size of our physical body is still with us, as part of our soul, until we learn to exist in the energy of the spirit world, and then we are seen as our innermost spirit. It is the *spirit* I painted of Gordon, still with certain recognisable features but mostly with the light, which is now him.

So, each part of your spirit has the potential to be drawn. Often people ask me to do this when they are in need of guidance as to their way forward spiritually. There may be a past life (part of the layers of their soul) which is holding them back and they need to acknowledge before they can move on. The readings are not prescriptive; in fact, when someone wants to have a soul portrait they will already have some spiritual knowledge and will be to be able to move their spiritual development forward.

Spirit portraits can take several forms ranging from angelic to divine and whatever else I can see in and around the sitter which I then draw and paint. On occasions I see off-earth entities in the spiritual aura of the sitter. I believe that; if our spirit is eternal and exists out of time and space then I have no problem with seeing an energy that is not humanoid. Some people may feel that to have an 'alien' in the spirit world is rubbish, but to me all impressions are acceptable and have a reason for being there.

Precognitive Art

Dunblane

I have said before that mediumship can be a blessings and a curse. Sometimes the experiences I have I wish I didn't have because they are so upsetting. I have asked my helpers and guides many times why I am given visions which relate to the future but because they can't be deciphered until the event, I am not able to do anything about the event. This brings to mind a very saddening experience I had where there was a loss of children. It happened when my daughter was between 5 and 6 years old. I awoke startled from a dream and asked my daughter if she was having PE or Gym that day in school because the dream was about school and children in a gym wearing the same red sweatshirts as my daughter. She said she didn't think she was but her gym kit was already in school. I dreamt that she was running around in a wooden floored hall, with the rest of her class all happy and enjoying the exercise. I could see her lovely blonde haired teacher who was blowing the whistle for the children to stop like statues, but, over the top of the children's giggling I heard a voice say 'Tom, don't do it, Tom!'

There was a boy in Becky's class called Tom, my friend's son, so I thought the shout referred to him as he was in the same class as my daughter.

I dreamed the dream at about 7.00am and then helped my family go off to school and to work. After they had gone and the house had quietened down I put the TV on in the background to catch the news. News Flash; 'Class full of children shot in a Dunblane Primary School, Scotland'! The assassin's name was Tom! I was dumbfounded and then I went into shock because I wanted to know why the spirit world had given me the dream too late for me to do anything about! I was so saddened about what had happened to the children that I began a painting-collage called 'Out of Chaos Comes Peace' which I sent to the school and received a letter back from them thanking me for the thought for the children.

I have often wondered why we have precognitive dreams and why are they given so late we can't do anything about them. My compassionate mind says that we need to stop these things happening, from floods and earthquakes to mass murder and war. But, why do we have to put our children through something like this? I think, in some ways, I am fortunate in that I can paint the impressions I receive and so it seems easier to adjust to the horror of what I see. The painting seems to reduce the blow of the visions. Below I have given a few of my examples of some of the many precognitive episodes I have had, some I have drawn and some I haven't, but all remain as 'real' in my mind as the moment I had them.

9/11

I was teaching one of my adult watercolour classes on the afternoon of the 11th September 2002. It was one of the first classes of the term and I was covering the basics of landscape painting. It was one of those classes when I was demonstrating how to paint the sky in the landscape and the watercolour paper, which should not buckle when wet, was not doing what it should do. As I was demonstrating how to paint the sky, using well tried and tested techniques, the paint was developing two long vertical, instead of horizontal, clouds in the sky. I tried dabbing off the paint to reduce the look of the vertical clouds but I couldn't do it. I ultimately laughed and said there were watercolour gremlins about and carried on the demonstration.

The time was about 2.00pm on the Monday afternoon. When I arrived home at just after three I switched on the TV just in time to see the twin towers in New York fall to leave these two vertical clouds just like the ones on the watercolour paper. Again shocked and bewildered that anyone could kill so many people I asked the spirit world why they show me things, on my watercolour paper, which I can't help with or stop happening.

Perhaps my answer came when I was asked to do a reading for a lady from a local University. A gentleman came, from spirit, to speak to her and said he was in the twin towers and could she tell his wife he loves her? The sitter said she knew of no one who was in the twin towers. The spirit gentleman said he worked at the University and was visiting New York when it happened. I did not want to push the point but a few days later she phoned me to say that there was a man at the University who died in the twin towers collapse and, although she did not know him she would try to get the message to his family.

There have been many occasions when I have seen disasters before they happen but I have never had an answer for why I see them other than I have then gone on to paint many of them. As well as drawing spirit portraits you may also have the ability to be shown visions of the type I have just spoken about. Once you have seen them it is up to you as to whether you want to draw or paint them. In my experience, drawing the vision helps expel the sight from the mind and so I don't carry it with me in my psyche.

Drawing a spirit portrait in watercolour

This is a photograph of Hollie which was given to me by her Grandmother after the demonstration of Spirit Art. The drawing was exhibited at the second Spirit Art Society exhibition in 2009 together with written and photographic evidence indicating the close likeness to Hollie.

Hollie (2009)
Pastel sketch completed during a demonstration of Spirit Art

Photograph of the German Grandfather emailed to me three weeks after
the demonstration by his Granddaughter

German Grandfather (2007)
Pastel sketch completed at a demonstration of Spirit Art in Darmstatt,
Germany

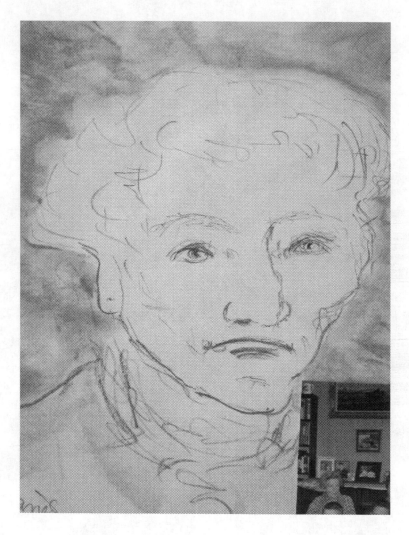

Mother-in-Law appears at Halfpenny Green Winery (2007)
Pastel sketch completed during a workshop at the vineyard

John
Sketched for his sister (2007) Pencil drawing completed during a private
sitting

An unexpected visitor helps at a workshop (2010) Pastel portrait of an
artist guide Anthony van Dyke

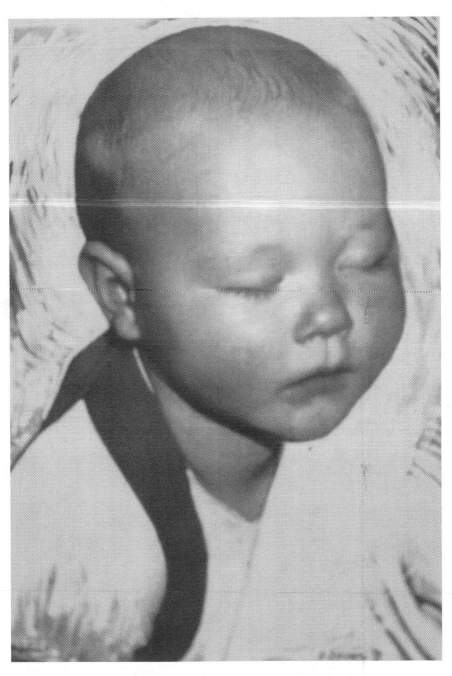

Dunblane : *Out of Chaos comes Peace* (1996)
Paper, ribbon and paint, photo-collage inspired by a dream

CREATING YOUR OWN
SPIRIT PORTRAITURE

down on paper and to know the difference between psychic and spirit art. Simply, psychic art uses earth bound psychic energies and so you will need to start by understanding the differences between the energy manifesting from yourself and those from the spirit world. Spirit art is about drawing energies which are not part of this solid physical life. It is different from psychic art and you will need to be a person who is a medium, or developing mediumship, in order to succeed at the higher levels of spiritual art.

I have found that many people, while studying on my spirit art courses, have found innate gifts which they then begin to use. So, try not to limit yourself, you never know what you can do if you don't try. The art and meditation exercises help you uncover skills in yourself which you may never have thought you had, however, these skills come with a need for an understanding of who and what you are drawing and painting through the nebulous connection with the spirit world. And all that comes with a need for a sense of responsibility towards, not only yourself, but also a consideration of that invisible world and the spirit people who abide there. We are not just communicating with our inner spirit but also the mind and soul of a person who had a physical life and body and who has since passed away, leaving their body behind and moving forward into a world of ether. It is that communication between your mind and the mind of a spirit which we, as spirit artists, connect with and, as in life, we need to be respectful of that person in spirit. I will be speaking more on this in the next chapter, let us first try to calm our mind.

Creating psychic and spirit art is not about how clever and graphically accurate the drawing are; it is about re-creating psychic, paranormal and spiritual sensation, experience and impression onto a drawing surface. As artists we look at a beautiful scene or flowers and we see the solid forms through our physical eyes and then the visual message of what we see is transferred to the brain, re-coded and then sent to the hand to draw or paint. When foot and mouth artists paint or draw, the visual 'message' is sent to the appropriate body-part working the drawing. We can, as artists, produce art work by seeing, by touching, by sensing, both physically and emotionally, and then recreate as drawings, paintings, sculptures, tapestries, feltings or in any other art form we wish to work in.

The seventeenth century artist William Blake (1757-1827) was said to be aware of the spirit world which he would then draw and illustrate in his work. Blake was not known to have been hallucinating through illness at the time nor under the influence of drugs or alcohol, which can trigger hallucinations, and so, it is thought, that what he painted was what he *saw* paranormally as manifesting beings. At the age of eight, after falling asleep in a London park, it is said that he woke to see cherubs flying around the top of the tree which, in his adult life as an artist, he went on to create as an etching. William Blake could be thought of as the first spirit artist since, although much of his work as an illustrator was drawn from the bible, he drew from visions he received while working on the illustrations he produced for his patrons.

Many artists create from impressions they feel internally about the person or scene they are looking at. Rolf Harris, a contemporary portraitist, said on a TV programme, while painting his portrait of Queen Elizabeth ll, "I am trying to capture the soul, or spirit of the Queen in this portrait". As an artist he was not only looking at the objective line, form, colour and physical make-up of the Queen but also how her personality came across to him which he attempted to create her on the canvas. Alan Stuttle, when teaching a psychic art class at the Arthur Findlay College of Psychic Studies, said; "All art is created through the soul of the artist, without soul art would be a dead thing". Here we have two artists speaking about similar activities while making their art, Alan, suggesting that art is created through the soul of the artist and Rolf trying to re-create the soul or life-force of his sitter.

Throughout history artists have pondered the same question. The agony and ecstasy of Michelangelo di Bonerotti who, while attempting to manifest, in paint, the image of God for the Sistine Chapel ceiling, questioned and queried within himself as to the authenticity of the image of the God he had painted: and also the wistful smile of *Mona Lisa* painted by Leonardo Da Vinci which has left many an art historian questioning who and why the portrait was painted. Similarly, a spirit artist will delve into the super-sensory impressions they receive in order to draw or paint that which they experience while manifesting their work. The only difference is, unlike a traditional artist, the spirit artist will be working with, mostly, *invisible* artefacts, landscapes and portraits which they then go on to paint.

Although there is no need to be able to draw in order to start creating psychic and spirit art there comes a point when the quality of drawing is affected if you can't. However, I tell my students that I have a 'foolproof' method of helping people draw a portrait, which I will be discussing later, so no-one should fail. Psychic art is mainly created using colour and symbols so to be good at drawing is not necessary. Spirit art, on the other hand, may take you into the technicalities of drawing portraits, landscapes and personal objects belonging to the person in spirit, so there will be a slightly higher level of expertise needed. Buying a good book on drawing may help, joining a drawing class at your local art college, taking a spirit art class with myself or using the two DVD's I have filmed based on the development of spirit and psychic art.

You may not need to be able to draw but in order to develop psychic art but you will need to have an understanding of the energies surrounding a person which I will discuss in the next chapter, and, you will need to know how to test the information you are receiving. The types of Psychic art consist of;

- Drawing and painting in paint or pastel the energies around people, animals and places
- Psychic auragraphs which includes psychic readings
- Drawing impressions received when in a landscape, building or touching objects gaining information regarding the energies closely attached to the place or object

Spirit art is about drawing and painting from spiritual manifestations such as visions, spirit sensations or automatically, i.e., allowing external spiritual influence determine what is being drawn. Often the latter type of art is created in a state of semi trance or overshadowing and is usually only obtained by an experienced medium.

So, there we have it. Developing psychic and spirit art should be developed in stages and by missing a stage it may mean you having to return to the stage missed later on in your developmental experience. It is best to work at each stage as it is in this book, practice and then go on to the next. That way you will have experienced all the stages. And, as I say in my DVD 'An Introduction to Psychic Development with Ann Davies' have fun and play with the process and techniques. Don't take it too seriously, the spirit world love mistakes and laughter.

Chapter Eight

CREATING SACRED SPACE

When creating spirit or psychic art the process is very different from other types of art, although, it could be said, that there are similarities with the drawing and painting techniques, but, there is no comparison with the use of psychic and spirit energy. It is not as though you can just sit down and draw the sitter or bowl of fruit in front of you because, unless you are a natural medium, communication with an invisible force needs to be developed and understood first. As an artist we have a place to work, sometimes in a studio and sometimes out in the field, with our art equipment around us. We make ourselves comfortable in order to begin the original artwork. As a psychic or spirit artist the same applies, that is, when you work, where you work and how you work, in order to create this type of art, matters a great deal. It is almost impossible to create psychic or spirit art in the middle of a busy studio or noisy place because there is a need to practice quietness and mediation within oneself first.

The quietness within is like being in meditation, or looking at a beautiful scene or being in a church. It is a sense of calm from inside you and outside you, almost like being at prayer when you feel at peace with the world. This sense of quiet has to be followed and learnt and used whenever a connection with the world of spirit or the invisible forces around a person are to be touched by you. Some people find this very easy and others, who are more naturally leading a fast or busy life can find this more difficult, however, it can be learnt and I will detail the methods by which you can achieve this inner calm later in this chapter.

Much has to do with the environment you are working in. A traditional artist can start their masterpiece in their purpose-built studio with all their art materials at hand. Most amateur artists will start their drawing or painting on the kitchen table with their materials to hand in a box, clearing and putting out the paper and materials whenever needed. Wherever you work and whatever you use to begin the psychic and spirit creative process the main ingredient is quiet and calm otherwise your creations will not be as good as they could be. When creating your space for working in you should keep this in mind so, if you have children in the home or noisy animals, you will need to work when either they are quiet or not at home. Animals do tend to feel the spiritual energies and can become calm, or perhaps go to sleep, but you really will need to be able to concentrate so if there is anything in the house which has the potential to disturb you, move it or yourself away from it.

When my daughter was small I would wait until she was in bed or in school before starting my spirit art commissions, and if there is a problem then I do not start. I wait for the house or room to become quiet again. I use my garage as a studio and in the winter I work inside where it is warmer. I make a space just for myself away from the computer or phone and try to keep that space only for the art work I am to do so if you have a spare room then make it into a small studio space which can be used both for readings or sittings for a spirit painting or pastel drawing.

The sacred space you create is so very important. It is almost a holy place. You should make it warm, calm and energised. Now, when an artist works, they naturally build up a creative energy just by concentrating on the art they are doing. Often they do not like to be disturbed when in the creative mood while you are working and nor should you. The energy you will need to build up in your sacred space is like being in a sacred place. While creating spirit artwork the sense of calm can be built up by playing meditation or new age music, the music can help to calm you as well as aid the ambience in the room or by meditating on calm and spiritual light there. It is a place which also calms the sitter when having a sitting and encourages the spirit world to come close to you.

My studio, where I create my own paintings as well as the spirit artworks, has music playing all the time. I have a particular piece of music which calms me and places me in the spirit art mood just by hearing it. It is not music with a pronounced beat or singing. It is music which flows. I could tell you what the piece is but that will not help you find the magic music which helps you. What I like may not relax you. The music should flow and if possible loop it so it can play for as long as you are working. When creating spirit artworks I can often 'go out of time and space'. I forget the time and it has gone dark outside when I think it is still 2.30 in the afternoon. This may not happen when you first begin to do the work but most certainly later. Artists when they are working often have this 'loss of time', or when a person is concentrating on a jigsaw or piece of knitting or even solving a mathematical puzzle, it is just how the mind works.

The importance of building a sacred space will become evident as you start to create as a medium or psychic or spirit artist. A small space away from the family, no matter how small it is, will work wonders to your artwork and concentration, and this is what matters. If you are one of those people who feels as though you always have got to be on the go meditation may not calm you at first, however, I always feel that if you practice the process of calming your mind, body and spirit in your sacred space before you start to do the meditation and then the psychic and spirit art, then the meditation will work.

So you have a special place to start your painting or drawing. This is the beginning of a wonderful journey. Make sure you have enough space to work in and to put the CD player or tape recorder, a table for your art equipment and something to lean your paper on. This can be a table or a small easel depending on how you like to work. When I am demonstrating spirit art I work at a large flip chart, when I have private readings I have a small easel, when I am painting large spirit landscapes I have a stand up easel and when I am lazy or there is nothing else I have a small table and, either have my art materials in a box to one side of the paper, laid out in pastel, pencil or paint order or, as I get going, sprawled all over the place.

Pastels get your hands, and materials, very dirty so try not to have a light coloured carpet or tablecloth because pastel dust gets everywhere including on your clothes and is not washed out easily. Wear dark clothing! These are only well experienced hints, eventually you will be working in your own way and in your own style so I will try not to be prescriptive or pedantic about what, where, how and when, you will work it out for yourself eventually. One more thing; the room needs to be as warm as you like it, not too hot and not to cold.

Once you have your space ready you will need to learn to relax in it. Use a meditation tape or easy listening music to place you in the right frame of mind. If your mind keeps wandering invest in one of my meditation CD's or DVD's, or even someone else's, because a spoken meditation which can take you on a journey may make you fall asleep but ideally will calm your mind. Sit in your sacred space and meditate as often as you can and when you feel ready to start to produce psychic art you will be calm and ready to do so.

Once you have mastered the relaxation of the mind you will be able to concentrate on your artwork which I will discuss in the next chapter. You will need to buy or retrieve from the bottom of an old drawer, or borrow from the children or grandchildren, the art materials which will be a necessary part of your advancement into creating psychic and spirit art. I suggest you do not buy expensive materials at first, in fact, I never have. My materials come from the cheapest shop and they have done me well for over 30 years, so try not to spend too much out on these, they can be expensive enough as it is. I will make a list below for you to decide if the art materials you already have are enough or whether you will need to buy some new art materials. I will list them in order of need, that is, the art equipment you will need to buy first so your financial outlay will not be too much when you first start.

Meditation Materials

* CD player
* Comfortable place to side for both you and the person you are sitting for

- Meditation CD or soft relaxing music
- Quiet room or space in which to work

Art Materials

- Paper for drawing no smaller than A4 size, A2 preferably. Not too smooth and the paper can be coloured but not too dark in shade unless you are working with white
- 2B pencil (if you look at the side of the pencil the quality is marked there)
- a cheap box of coloured pastels
- pencil sharpener, or sharpening knife; but because the knife can be considered dangerous make sure the children don't get hold of it
- pastel eraser or putty eraser (putty rubber)

As you advance;

- watercolour box (not tubes yet)
- wax crayons especially white
- charcoal pencils
- better pastel paper or Ingres paper
- sizes 2,4 and 6 or 8 non-natural-hair watercolour paint brush or thin, medium and thick watercolour paintbrush
- water carrier or jam jar
- watercolour paper, no lighter than 140 lbs in weight or 300 grms in weight (this can be expensive)
- field easel (optional)

As you become experienced;

- pastel paper
- A2 size watercolour paper
- Stretched canvas
- Acrylic paints
- Acrylic paint brushes
- Digital camera and computer
- Palette knives
- Stand up easel

And, anything else you would like to draw with, for example, Chinese brushes, twigs, cotton buds, cling-film, alcohol (for mark-making and painting not for drinking) inks, charcoal etc.

At some point all the equipment will be used but because you don't know if you are going to take to this type of artwork it is best not to spend too much at once. There are people I have taught who only work with the beginners set of art equipment and do a very good job of it. I'm not really a skinflint, I am just very practical. Sometimes less is more and when you first begin it is wise not to have too much to confuse the making of your unique artwork.

OK, you have built your sacred space; you have placed all the equipment you will need in the best place for you. You have the relaxing music playing and you are ready to go! You sit on the lovely chair which you have put in the best place in your work room, the music is playing and you feel lovely and chilled and you close your eyes drifting into a wonderful place of peace. Two minutes into the meditation you realise you have forgotten something because you are suddenly, abruptly, shocked out of your slumber by the telephone ringing. Can't do much about the doorbell, but the telephone can be switched to mute or the dog blanket placed over it!

Psychic and spirit art must be created in a place of quiet and peace at first. You need the best place to work and a telephone ringing will not help that. Try to remember to switch it off or turn the sound down. Give yourself 20 to 40 minutes at first, which may be difficult for some when you start, but you will soon sink into a routine. You will experience some problems with your meditation at first and it might be that you need to be guided in a meditation to start with either by joining a class or using an already mastered CD which will lead you in and out of meditation.

Once you become experienced at moving in and out of psychic consciousness you will be able to create the psychic or spirit art, as I do, in the middle of a group of people or while teaching. The process of going into meditation is the same as changing your consciousness. In meditation some people talk about going downwards and some people say they go up. Some people fall asleep and others can hear a pin drop in another room. Everybody is different but the one thing in common is that they all feel relaxed (sometimes spaced out) and energised. If you feel dizzy when you come back into the room then you are not grounding yourself when you come out of the meditation and you should consciously bang your feet and clap your hands and have a drink of water when you do emerge out of the meditation to ground yourself. If the dizziness continues you will need something to eat and if it continues after that then it is not the meditation it will be a problem you already have. Go and see your doctor. I advise you to take a few weeks to enhance and get used to the change in your consciousness during your meditation before you begin drawing, it will make a difference when you ultimately start to create your masterpieces.

During mediation practice there is always a change in consciousness. When we fall asleep we have a change in consciousness from shallow to deep sleep, so, there is nothing to be concerned about regarding a change in how you feel and if this does concern you then join a meditation class. It is possible to do the exercises without meditating but the depth of understanding is different if there is not a change. Some people say it is like being at prayer or very, very, calm so the best advice I can give is try a little at a time until you become more experienced.

Your room or sacred space is ready, you have all the materials and now you are ready. Ask yourself if you really want to do this. If you want to make creations which will develop your mediumship, your creativity and your personal sense of well being. You will be taught to draw portraits and spiritual landscapes and you will be taken to your Temple of Light in the invisible world of spirit. The journey will be exciting. You will want to stay with one or two of the exercises more than others and you can work entirely at your own pace, time and who with. This is your journey and your journey alone when your creativity and sensitivity will be heightened. Are you ready to take on the challenge?

The next chapter is about the process, techniques and methodology of psychic and spirit art and you will be asked to complete an exercise at a time. It is important not to skip an exercise as they are designed to develop your skills at the right pace remembering we are working with both the psyche and creativity. Enjoy each step and get as much out of it as you can. Most of the exercises can be done by anyone and there is no artistic skill needed. I will take you through them step by step so you can understand and enjoy each move of the pencil, pastel or brush. Keep your equipment at the ready, you never know when you will feel inspired to draw or paint.

If you are already an artist the art work exercises may seem child-like to you and the meditation hard, and, if you are used to meditating and not an artist you may find the artwork more difficult to do, either way, I suggest you work through the practices and exercises step by step as you may find you learn more along the way than you originally thought.

Chapter Nine

WHAT IS THE DIFFERENCE BETWEEN
SPIRIT ART AND PSYCHIC ART?

Spirit and psychic art are not only about the drawing and painting of portraits, personal objects and landscapes of the mostly unseen invisible spirit world of the afterlife; it is also about the development of the self. Without the creation of a bridge between our higher self, the spirit body, and our incarnate mind we would not be able to make a firm connection with our artist guides and teachers who wish to help us start creating our artworks. Of course the best people to speak to about this cross-over of communication between the two worlds are people who call themselves mediums.

From a very young age I have been able to draw what I see in the after-life. I am what is known as a *natural* medium. According to Spiritualists those who have the faculty of being able to communicate with spirit are known as mediums and they have abilities known as clairvoyance, clairaudience and clairsentience, that is, they are able, with or without fore-thought, to see, hear or sense the spirit energies of those who are no longer alive in the physical world. They are either born with the prerequisite facility in place or they have developed it through a variety of means. Mediums say that they can communicate with those in what they think of as the world of spirit which is apparently devoid of matter.

There also seems to be a difference between those who have psychic abilities and those who have ability to communicate with a deceased person, the details of which I will discuss later; also, in order to reflect this difference, there is a difference between the art created and known as psychic art and the art known as spirit art. As a natural medium I am both psychic and mediumistic. To explain this I need to explain the qualities of these two types of paranormal activity.

To begin; in order to understanding of the concept and process of psychic development and mediumistic development we will need to understand that we, who are alive and in a physical body, have a spirit, which can also be called a soul or mind which resides, while we are alive, as part of, but also distinct from, our physical body, and it is this spirit mind which communicates with the afterlife. It is this mind, body, spirit concept which we use when creating spirit art, and, although, within spiritualist circles, there is a belief that there is no need to totally understand or have a belief in the afterlife in order to create spirit art, just as you don't have to be an artist to create a portrait. However, the ins and outs of the concept of an afterlife still need to be referred to in order to classify the two distinct types of art.

What are these two types of art and how do spirit and psychic artists produce them? It is understood by mediums and psychics that the physical body has an energy which is known by those who can see or sense this energy as pranic energy or 'life force' and this energy, while the body is alive, manifests as an electromagnetic 'aura' around the physical body. It is this aura which a psychic can see or sense and can also penetrate to 'read' when reading a person's physical and, or, emotional health and the mental and, or, spiritual, ability. This invisible-to-most energy is the individual's life force, made up of the above, and which has been studied by several religions or beliefs for thousands of years. A psychic can read these energies and translate them into a reading to give the person receiving the message, the recipient of the message. It is believed, by those who are supernaturally sensitive, that all human beings are psychic and some animals too, so, it is believed that we all have the innate ability to be psychic.

How often have we thought about someone and the telephone rings or we get an email from them? This type of telepathic communication can be psychic. When we enter a room we may find that we don't like the 'vibes' (vibrations) in that room and would like to leave as soon as possible. Our husband or friend may wonder what we are talking about and to them there is nothing wrong with the room. It may be that the couple living there have just had an argument and it is the remnants of the angry energy which has built up, and which the person who wants to leave may be sensing because they are sensitive to those particular energies in the room. The person is picking that energy up psychically. Take this one stage further and the same person could dowse the energies around a person (with their permission) and give them a reading on what they find. This type of energy-reading of rooms, landscapes, people and houses is a psychic activity.

The difference between a reading which has been made psychically, and one which has been made with some sort of communication from the afterlife, is that the psychic reading is based on that which is physically manifesting around that person within their physical aura. A medium, on the other hand, can do the same but will also sense, at a different vibrational frequency, the energies of those who have died and their energies departed the physical world. The medium *tunes* into those who have only the spirit mind or soul body, with which to communicate. A well know analogy of this 'tuning in' is that of a ham radio operator and if you are as old as I am, you will remember the noise from the radio when it wasn't properly tuned and as you turned the dial the speaker's voice would fade in and fade out. Mediumship is very similar; we tune our vibrations in and out of the higher vibrations of the spirit world, by changing our consciousness, in order to achieve communication with them. This method of communication is called mediumship and the other, when dealing purely with physical energies, is usually known as psychism.

It is important to understand the difference between the two because, it is believed that, when a reader is dealing only with the physical earth energies of a person they can only make connections with the person's past and present whereas a medium is said to be able to connect with the future, as well as the past and present, because they are communicating with a spirit, in a world with apparently no time and space, who can witness the future as well as the past. Understandably, these types of readings must be treated with care and responsibility because as mediums and psychics we can influence other peoples' lives which are why any communication received either psychically or spiritually must be treated with respect.

After a demonstration of spirit art when I have drawn 5 or 6 spirit portraits I have had people say that when they receive a verbal message from a medium the recipient of the message sometimes does not really know who the medium is communicating with and who the medium says it is? Sometimes the same information can fit two loved ones or friends. Sometimes there can be confusion as to who the spirit communicator is, because the spirit person hasn't been very clear with their information or the medium hasn't been able to receive much information from them. However, I have often been told after demonstrations of spirit art that with a spirit portrait the proof is there in front of them, in a solid form, and a photograph can usually be produced to prove the portrait is who I or the spirit communicator say they are. I feel that spirit art is so important to mediumship, and proof of the afterlife, because the portraits speak for themselves and can be shown to be who the spirit people say they are, especially when the message and the drawing fit the criteria of the spirit person in the drawing.

Psychic and spirit art are therefore different in methodology, technique and process. There are also different classifications of spirit art some of which are dated as far back as man began drawing in caves, but the more recent paintings were created in the mid nineteenth century USA. In a small purpose built town in northern New York state called Lily Dale. It was here that two sets of mediums were producing, apparently through physical mediumship, oil and pastel paintings by telekinesis. These precipitated paintings were usually portraits of spirit guides and spirit loved ones.

Lily Dale Assembly was a summer home for many mediums from the late nineteenth century and people interested in the supernatural could visit or stay for a holiday and have readings with recognised and well vetted mediums or soak in the spiritually charged environment. This is where the Bangs sisters and the Campbell 'Brothers' lived and worked in the summer months between 1893 and 1926. The Bangs sisters May and Elizabeth (Lizzie) would sit with a person, in an empty room, except for a table, some chalk pastels, a Bristol board and chairs. The person who wanted a reading from them would sit and watch as a pastel portrait would materialise on a paper board in a matter of minutes, like a photograph developing, much to the amazement of the sitters. Likewise, the Campbell brothers, (Allen Campbell and Charles Shourds) would create large canvas oil paintings and some pastel portraits, of guides and loved ones for the sitters often in Town halls or theatres around America as well as Lily Dale.

Many of the spirit produced precipitated paintings, from both sets of mediums, were created, completely hands free by these four mediums and have not been produced since. After the death of Charles Shourds, in 1926, the last precipitation medium at Lily Dale, the ability to manifest these paintings seemed to die with him. However a new form of spirit art began to be created in England by Frank Leah, a competent artist in his own right, who in the 1930-40's became interested in theosophy and spiritualism and began to draw the portraits of the invisible spirit people who visited him in his studio after seeing them clairvoyantly. It is from his work that most of the spirit artists of today have come from because much of the spirit art now, like his, is being produced for evidential reasons, that is, to prove a life after death.

Coral Polge, Ivor James, Alan Stuttle, and I all became interested in spirit art after either seeing one of the early artists at work or joining a course at the Arthur Findlay College of Psychic Studies, the Greater World Association, The Theosophist Society or the Society for Psychical Research. Mediumship was illegal in Britain until the 1950's and if an artist was producing spirit art it was either under cover behind locked doors or as part of a larger organisation. Spirit art has been with us in Britain for over a century and is still little known.

Under the classification of psychic art are all the drawings, paintings and sketches which are created using only the paranormal energies of the recipient, i.e.; auragraphs which are symbolic representations of the recipient, drawings or paintings based on the representation of the life force energy around a person sometimes used for healing diagnosis, and any other form of art which comes from the reading or sensing of the energies of a living person or animal. These can be created on any paper with any art materials, any size or structure.

On the other hand spirit art would include drawings and paintings of portraits, landscapes or object drawing which are personal to the spirit of a deceased person, such as; a portrait of a deceased person, drawings of the home they lived in or the work they did or the objects they owned. For example, a watch or brooch or article of clothing which can give evidential information regarding the deceased person. Of course, to prove evidence of the afterlife, the artist should have no prior knowledge of the spirit person. Spirit drawings and paintings can be mastered using any art material to any size and can be worked either clairvoyantly, clairsentiently, clairaudiently, automatically (automatic drawing) or through physical mediumship when the artwork is produced solely by the spirit world using the energy of the physical medium in order to create the picture.

Psychic art, because there is a belief that all living beings are psychic, can be created by anyone who is interested in psychic matters, whereas, spirit art always needs the abilities of a medium who can see, sense or hear the spirit world as part of the process of creation. Later in the chapter I will be giving exercises in how to develop these abilities. You never know what may come about in starting to draw with the power of spirit.

In 2007 I was asked to demonstrate spirit art in a theatre in West Kirkby, near Liverpool, for a cancer charity. At that meeting I was to work longer than usual so I had decided to show the audience the difference between psychic art and spirit art. After being introduced by the organisers I gave a short explanation of what I was about to do that evening and asked if there was a member of the audience who would like to come up onto the stage for me to draw.

With sepia conte crayon I began drawing the portrait of the young lady who had ventured onto the stage and explained what I was doing as I went along. The audience was attentive and hushed which was a sign that they were interested in what I was doing. The drawing took shape, long light coloured hair flowing around the girl's shoulders. After a few minutes I began drawing coloured lines around the head, face and figure not quite obliterating the original drawing. I explained that I was drawing the young lady's aura which was an invisible energy around her body, above her head and below her feet. I was inspired by the flow of colours all around her.

Some of the shapes I could see with my clairvoyant vision and some I sensed clairsentiently.

I explained and described what I was doing as I was working the drawing and then I said to the lady that I sensed dullness around her left ear where I had drawn a little grey cloud and asked her if she had problems with her hearing on the left side. She gasped and said she had had an accident when she was a child and she had hearing problems on that side. I pointed to a variety of colours, interpreted the colours and then asked her if what I was saying about her personality, love life and schooling were correct. She said they were and that all I had said was one hundred percent accurate. I asked her if she knew what I was doing and she said that she had never heard of an aura but she was able to sense things around people and sometimes got headaches which weren't hers. The young lady was obviously psychic and, when looking at the bright yellow and lilac around her head, these colours are usually an indication of mediumship too. Interpretation of these colours meant that her psychic experience was still quite immature but could be advanced with a good book on mediumship or teacher.

On that occasion the reading was very positive but sometimes when I see peoples' auras I would not want to discuss what I see in front of an audience because what I see may not be as positive, I have to decide what to say at the time. It was just the right time and place for the young lady to receive the information she did at that time. That night I carried on to demonstrate spirit portraiture to the audience showing them the difference between the psychic drawings and the spirit ones creating about six spirit portraits That particular evening of mediumship was a lovely occasion when everybody seemed to enjoy themselves and because I explained what I was doing all the way through, they went home having learnt the difference between the two methods.

Psychic drawings can be very valuable in helping people understand themselves. A psychic who links into the auric body of a person can sense certain impressions from the person's energy field. These impressions, which I have discussed above, can be quite personal. When I was in my twenties I was visiting a friend in Bath in the south of England and because it was a lovely summery evening we decided to go to the local pub for a drink. We walked into a bistro type bar and my friend noticed a few of her colleagues sitting by the window. Now, because this was many, many years ago in my youth, I cannot remember how the conversation came around to fortune telling but my friend suggested I look into the girl's hand. The girl thrust her hand towards me and, as I closed the hand, I said, 'no, I don't do that sort of thing', she pulled her hand back and said, you're the second person who wouldn't read my hand, the first said I would have an unexpected death!' I was shocked to hear her say that and tried to explain that I was not going to say that to her, but she would not listen. However what I had felt when I touched her hand was a feeling of great sadness and remorse which was not the same as death.

We quickly left the pub and never spoke of it again. However, the memory never left me because this is an example of inappropriate time and place for psychic readings. I had not asked to read her hand, it was thrust on me and often in those circumstances words can be said which are not right and this scenario should be avoided at all costs. I think the phrase goes; 'Loose lips sink ships'. A reading is a very emotive and personal experience both for the reader and the psychic so, when asked to do a reading on the spot, choose your words and place carefully, often the reading is never forgotten, especially when it has been anticipated for a long time.

Another memory I would like to share with you regarding an inappropriate psychic reading was many years ago when I was taken to an outdoor market that had stalls selling everything under the sun, including chickens and live-stock. One of the stalls took my attention, the stallholder was selling old-fashioned bric-a-brac and there was a row of handy-man's tools laid out on the green velvet cloth. My father used to have tools just like them and as I stretched out to pick one of the shiny screwdrivers up I developed a sharp stabbing pain under my ribs. I kept hold of the screwdriver to look at it but my breath was being taken away by the pain. I must have looked peaky because the stall-holder asked if I was feeling all right. I said I wasn't and could do with a drink of water.

She went off and brought back a paper cup filled with tap water and suggested I put the screwdriver down. Shortly after I let it go of the screwdriver the pain went from my side and I thought it was due to having been a little bit dehydrated and the water relieved the pain. Apparently not! The stall holder began to tell me the story of how she obtained the screwdrivers. A young man stole the screwdrivers many years ago from a neighbour. That night he took one of them into town and stabbed another young man under the ribs who ultimately died. After the police had done with them, (this was a time before police forensic evidence sciences we have today, were available) they were returned to the owners who never used them again. When the owner died, himself of old age, she was given them to sell.

What had happened was that the screwdriver had been left with the residual psychic energy from the stabbing impressed on it and I inadvertently 'picked up' the pain of the assault up when I touched the object. This form of psychic sensitivity is called psychometry and the police have been using psychics and this technique for many years to find people and solve crimes. The impression the psychic received from the objects are believed to provide missing information for the police to use; however, the information is not generally used in a court of law because it cannot be proven. So, I had unwittingly received an impression from the screwdriver and this is one reason why I don't buy second-hand goods unless I know where and from whom they have come from.

Psychic awareness can be a blessing and a curse because as it is developed it is more than just screwdrivers we can gain impressions from. Friends, family, neighbours have all got living auric energy around them and so it is best to close off your energies as much as possible otherwise you may be tuning into every Tom, Dick or Harry, object or animal without knowing it. You may think the headache is yours but try giving it back to the young man who lives across the road after having had a good night out last night! One way to reduce the exposure to psychic energy is to draw it. With an in breath feel the energy and with an out breath sketch the colour, form and consistency of the impression.

Psychic art is all about drawing and painting earth bound energies. Any energy which can be seen heard or felt using paranormal methods. The same process is used when drawing an aura of a person or the energy from a rock or piece of land. You will use the same techniques of 'linking-in' to the energies and then offload onto your paper, board or canvas in the form of a drawing or painting.

Spirit art, on the other hand, is to do with non earth energies and they fall into three types; clairvoyant, automatic and energetic using non-physical energy. These three types connect with the spirit world in different ways. A clairvoyant artist will see the spirit world through their 'third eye' and transfer what they see onto the work surface. The images can be of faces, people, animals, memory objects and landscapes and are distinct from visionary art which may originate from the subconscious. Clairvoyant images should always come from images projected to us from the spirit world as distinct from visions and hallucinations. This is a concept which is very difficult to contextualise. Clairvoyance, clairsentience and clairaudience all seem to work together, albeit in different proportions, when producing mediumistic images and they can be created by using any art process while the medium is the artist drawing the impressions received from the after-life.

Automatic drawing is different from clairvoyant art because the medium is not necessarily the artist. The medium offers the use of their body in the creation of the artwork. When demonstrating spirit art to an audience when I am also giving verbal evidence of the spirit being drawn, I offer the use of my hand to the spirit artist to use bypassing my own ability as an artist. My understanding of this is that the spirit artist will trigger the part of my brain which operates my hand. The spirit artist then draws the image for me and during a demonstration this will take no more than 2 minutes to complete, usually taking less time, then I finish off the details clairvoyantly.

I have drawn hundreds of portraits in this way during many demonstrations and each one is different. I have found that if I interfere with the drawing while it is being created the drawing is not as accurate an evidential picture. That is, as an evidential portrait it is not as good. The nose may be too wide or long or the features are wrong, so my aim when drawing automatically is not to get in the way by staying slightly to one side of my physical body while the drawing is being done. I have been doing this a long time and feel safe working this way. After the drawing is complete I will then give the verbal evidence, for example, of who the person may be, what they died of and the work they did while alive, or the relationship to the recipient of the drawing. Once identified as being an accurate representation of the face o a spirit person then my job is done.

I have seven or eight spirit artists working with me when I work automatically. These artist guides are both men and women all of whom were artists in their own right while alive. Some like to work in pastel and some in watercolour or ink and I can usually tell who the artist is by the art materials they choose to work with while drawing. There is also a gentleman who draws cartoon portraits, so when the portrait looks like a cartoon I know it is him doing it. As an artist I have often asked myself why I don't get on developing my own style of art instead of allowing other artists to work through me; I am glad to have the choice to be able to do both. I feel I was born to do what I do and I can't complain about that.

The third method of creating spirit art is by physical mediumship, whereby the medium does not touch the paper, board or canvas at all and leaves the drawing up to the spirit world. I have not created artwork by this method yet but I am working on it. In order to create this sort of artwork there is a need for strong paranormal energy and the closest I have been to doing this is when I moved a pencil across a table using energy alone and creating portraits in teacups with the left over tea. Yes this does sound strange but at the end of every meditation my group has a cup of tea and on many occasions I have found that the residue at the bottom or side of the cup has dried in the shape of a face, once the shape was the face of a dog and once it was in the shape of my granny's face. This is an area I am working on and hope that one day I may produce some precipitated paintings like the Bangs Sisters in Lily Dale.

I have recently been working on a series of images on canvas which are based on energy. Using the colour impressions, as a basis to the work, I gather the paint in my hand and allow the colour to transfer from my hands onto the canvas without looking. I feel the energy, I feel the colour and I transfer the impression onto the work surface. My painting *The Void* came out of this process and method. The painting, when standing in front of it, gives out energy even without you looking at it. As I painted the spirit-scape I could feel spiritual energy flow out of my hands onto the canvas and it seems this is what gives the painting its 'power'. When people who are sensitive to energies stand in front of it they can feel dizzy with the flow of energy.

Ann Bridge Davies

The paintings are produced while in a semi trance state and are the next stage to automatic drawing. Instead of a spirit artist creating the drawings or paintings my own spirit takes over and brings through the energy which is then transferred to the painting surface. Often the paintings created by this method are large in size and painted in acrylic on canvas. The larger the better, however, since I am only just five foot in height, any larger than my height is impractical when working in a small studio. I have the paints and water ready and to hand, then wearing a pair of surgical gloves in order to save my hands from any damage from the paint or surface; I tune into my higher self and begin painting. I am usually not aware of what I am doing for a short time. It is rare for me to be painting for longer than half and hour and, anyway, I am tuned out by the spiritual forces around me as the process comes to an end. From these paintings, when dry, often emerge faces and animal shapes as though the spirit world have been moving the paint about before it dries using the surface energy resting on the canvas.

I really love creating this type of art because for me it is like a meditation in itself. I suppose it is a little like what the whirling dervishes do when they spin in their meditation. I am often amazed at the energy which pours out of the canvas months after the painting is completed. I wonder, what is next for spirit art?

134

Chapter Ten

DEVELOPING MEDIUMISTICALLY AND CREATING YOUR OWN SPIRIT PORTRAITS

I have written this chapter in such a way as to help you start your drawing with exercises that non artists and artists alike can do. For some of the exercises you will need another person to help, or, for you give readings to, and in other exercises you will have free rein, either way, the exercises are laid out as a 'step by step' guide to develop the use of the art materials, spiritual energies and your inner self so that you can ultimately give mediumistic readings together with spirit or psychic art. In this chapter we look at how to create a sacred space in which to meditate and produce the art work. This space should be available before we start creating our art work because as soon as we begin to get that urge to paint or draw the equipment should be ready.

In understanding that psychic art is created from the energies of others the following three simple exercises should help you develop your own awareness of the spirit and psychic energies which are around the person you are reading for. I have set the tasks in such a way as to 'step-up' the psychic energy as you go from one to the next and I suggest you do one at each sitting until you are familiar with the methods, process and materials you are using. Also, becoming familiar with the auric energies around a person is an important aspect to the development of the art. Each and every person is different and so each and every aura will be different in a psychical, mental, emotional and spiritual way.

Having taught these three simple exercises in workshops for many years I have found that, just as artists have their own style, so will you. Your psychic art will be different for each reading because the impressions you receive from the person whose energy passes through your aura are unique to each person. You may use bright bold colours for one whereas the next person you may use pale colour hues; you may favour large paper and pastels, whilst another person's reading will be created in watercolour with mixed media. Play with the materials and ask your inner self which art materials and colours to use if you doubt yourself.

How To Start?

To start with you have built your sacred space. This is a place where you will build up spirit energy, meditate and create your artwork. In order to build your sacred space allow the paranormal energies which are manifesting around you to built up by filling the space with golden light until you feel the room is energised. You may want to ask a guide or angel to help you keep the room positive and recharged after each sitter. You should develop your inner calm before each reading and then call the person into your sacred space. They too will feel the change in energy and calm in the room. You may want to have relaxing music in the background to keep up the calm ambience, it is up to you.

The exercises below are a basic introduction to psychic art and once you have worked through the three exercises, develop some of your own, and keep practicing until you have the understanding and knowledge to move forward onto spirit art. After doing the exercises I suggest you keep a log or journal as to your feelings, comments, results and anything else you want to write or draw in your journal so you can look back on it later. Your first attempts may be good or bad, but even so, write the impressions down to help you understand the process and to give a history of the impressions and ideas of that you liked, didn't like and couldn't understand then but will later.

When you begin to do readings, based on psychic and spirit art, the mediumistic information which you receive is either from the *recipient* in the case of psychic art, or from the *spirit world* in the case of spirit art and you need to know the difference between the two energies. The artwork is a message in itself and, sometimes, not an artistic masterpiece. However, as you practice and begin manifesting the higher levels of spiritual inspiration, the drawings, paintings and messages begin to reflect this and the artwork become masterpieces in their own right. Some spirit artists do not sign their work, personally I sign and date any art I do so I can look back on the development I have made and I make the joke that, "When I die, and return to the mysterious world of spirit, my drawings and paintings will be worth… who knows…maybe nothing!" The preparation below will be repeated at each session when you start to create psychic art, so I will describe now how to begin for this exercise only and then you should do the same each time you do a reading. The materials and sitter will change but the process of linking into the energies of the sitter should stay the same. For all three psychic art exercises you will need someone to read for, that is, a friend or family member who will be the recipient of the picture and message and will be honest with you regarding your delivery.

Psychic Art

Focusing or Scrying

For this exercise you will need; your journal, a graphite pencil and some white paper, one sheet for you to write your psychic impressions on and another to draw on for the person you are reading for. This is a two way exercise and the recipient of your reading must be assured that the information you have received from their aura is both confidential and important. While reading you will be receiving information regarding their history and private life so the recipient in each of the exercises must feel confident that what is said in the room stays in the room. You, and only you, are responsible for all you say to a person in a reading.

Exercise One

1. Ask your sitter to draw a circle on the piece of paper. This circle does not have to be perfectly round; this is all part of the reading.

2. Ask the sitter to shade in the circle without thinking about the drawing, stress that they should think about their life or other things but not the drawing. Some close their eyes so they don't interfere with the essence of the drawing. The reason why they should not concentrate is because some sitters can influence, subconsciously, how they are shading the circle in and so interfere with the reading. What you are looking for in the shading is information from the consciousness of the person. Some people like to 'get things right' and shade the circle in perfectly which does not help you as the reader. The end product, the drawing should look like a ball of wool the kitten has taken around the room - a lot of scribble. This should only take a matter of seconds.

3. In the scribble you will find clues to the physical, emotional and spiritual outlook of the person. What I mean by that is; it is your turn now as the psychic reader to scry into the scribble and find clues which relate to the life of the person. Turn the paper, look beyond that which is first evident, can you see letters, numbers, objects, faces?

4. On a separate piece of paper write down what you can see, decide if there are time levels indicated in the sketch? What else can you see? It is a black and white image, can you see colour? Write everything down.

5. Now the reading. You can tell the recipient what you see but the reading starts when you begin to interpret the images you could see in the scribble. This is a little like the lady who reads the crystal ball, she seems to be looking a nothing but glass, but within the glass the lady would be able to see shapes and forms, which she then speaks about.

6. The reading is about the impressions you sense from the things you have seen, this is where responsibility comes in. Just as when a reader reads the Tarot cards and the death card comes up he or

she would not automatically say there was going to be a death, there may be other reasons for this card such as a complete change in life or job or relationship. So the impressions received from the scribble (which is an indication of what the recipient has in their past and present history) give you clues as to who the people are around them, what sort of job they may have, what they like to eat, etc. Take care not to make things up, but do go with your inner instincts, after all you are working from a psychic standpoint and if the impressions you are receiving feel good then say so. All this takes practice and this is why you do this for people you know before people you don't know.

7. Deliver the reading from the apparent scribble in good faith. If you see a letter, for example the letter W, what can this mean? Is it the name of someone around the recipient or a deceased member of the family, perhaps William, a grandfather? Try to surmise this from the drawing first rather than ask the person. This is how you learn, and often by, at first, getting it wrong.

8. After interpreting the scribble try to sum up the reading. Bring the whole lot to a conclusion and allow the recipient to respond to you, either by saying that they understood nothing or they could understand parts or the whole lot. We learn by getting it wrong as well as getting it right so don't be disheartened when the reading does not go well, just try again.

9. What you will need is practice. You may think that the artwork in this exercise is babyish and not art at all, but after writing your comments in your journal, put it away and then a few weeks later read the comments again, you will see how much you have learnt which will encourage you to do more.

Once you feel you have succeeded in the first task go onto the second. You will find it easier especially if you have kept up your daily meditations. In your journal draw any unusual things which happen in your meditations because you may find that once you start to draw your first spirit art the impressions you receive in the early stages will not make sense to you. Try not to run before you can walk. With all paranormal activities the supernatural energies have to 'sit in'. That is; you have to get used to the changes in your own development just as the energies, especially those from the spirit world, have to respond to you. When you feel ready, start to practice Exercise Two which will take you to a slightly higher vibration within the aura of the person you are reading.

Exercise Two

Graphing the aura

For this exercise you will be drawing an auragraph by making a link with someone you are looking at or creating a picture for. You will need; your journal, a pencil, chalk pastels and size A3 white paper. Prepare your inner self as you did with Exercise One and when you feel relaxed and have that sense of inner calm then we can ask the sitter to enter your sacred space and begin the reading.

1. Ask your sitter to take a piece of white paper and draw around one of their hands and the lower part of their arm on the paper. The fingers should be relaxed and slightly spread out. The sitter should concentrate and try to send their energy into the drawing as they draw around the hand. It does not matter if the drawing is clumsy, you will be working over it in coloured pastels.

2. Take the pencil outline drawing of the sitter's hand and place it in front of you. As you look at the drawing you may already see, paranormally, faint almost invisible colours inside or around the hand, take a note of these colours on another piece of paper and place your hand over the drawn hand of the sitter about and inch away. You will start to paranormally feel the energy of the sitter's aura which they will have put into the drawing and you may clairvoyantly start to see colours or symbols. Take your hand away and start to draw the symbols and colour in the impressions you have received directly onto the drawn hand.

3. Every sitter's energy is different and so for one person you may sense an aggressive or active energy. Choose the colours you think represent that feeling. You may on the other hand, sense a soft but powerful energy which impress's you to use more gentle colours

and shapes. Create that flow between you and the sitter through the drawing and gradually build up a hand graph of the sitter's energy.

4. In this exercise you will be sensing at a slightly higher level than the first one. This is because you are linking more directly to the person's mental, emotional and physical well being and you may find you want to talk about their state health or well being.

5. If you draw symbols work out what they mean and jot the explanations down in your journal. For example if you sense and draw a new key then the person may be moving house or job and there is a new pathway for them. If it is an old key you have sensed in their auric field then this maybe something coming up from the past. It is your decision as to what your symbols and colours mean.

6. I have deliberately left out a section on symbols and colours because I feel you should build up an alphabet to your own meanings to symbols and colours. If you get stuck you can always search the internet for someone else's view but your own instinctive impression is usually the best to go by.

7. Once you have completed drawing your impressions of colours, symbols or objects then you can begin the interpretation. I suggest that if you do receive any impressions of ill health you should speak about them very carefully. As I have said before, and stress again, you are in a position or responsibility to your sitter and anything you receive should be taken seriously but offered with sensitivity, care and in confidence. We are not doctors or medical professionals and so should not diagnose. The person you are reading for may already know of ill health so if they offer the information that should be acceptable to the reading. At first your impressions will be quite simple but as you practice this exercise you will find you receive more and more information some of which may reach into a spiritual reading but at first most of the information will be of a psychic nature while you link psychically into the energy field of another.

8. This exercise can be done in several different ways. You can also draw a stick person on the paper, or if more able to draw, the figure of a person, and sense the energies around the sitter then draw a full aura for the sitter. This is very valuable for those who are on the path of spiritual healing because you will still be able to sense at several different levels the auric field of the person which you can then draw. Start with the physical aura, then the mental aura, then the emotional body then, if you feel you can, and with some practice, the spiritual colours of the person.

9. You can also draw the graphs of the aura for animals and places if you want to take this exercise further. You may find you produce some really interesting drawings and paintings from doing this exercise.

10. Take care not to do too much at once. As you develop your psychic awareness and mediumship each sphere of development must be understood before going on to the next otherwise little bits of understanding regarding psychic energies may not be fully understood. When you feel ready go onto the next exercise.

Exercise Three

Auragraphs

For the exercise you will need; your journal and all your art materials to hand. Choose the best paper for the exercise, either coloured or white pastel paper if working in pastels, or watercolour paper if working in watercolours. You may wish to start with just paper and pencils for the first attempt and then work up to pastels and watercolours and keep your mind open to using a variety of art materials. Again start in the same way as you have earlier making sure you are in calm and receptive frame of mind before you start.

1. In this exercise you will be producing drawings or paintings of a full aura-graph. Ask your sitter to enter your sacred space and explain what you are going to do. Describe to your sitter that you are going to dowse their auric energy field and psychically receive impressions of objects, times, animals, places, people and, or, landscapes which

will have something to do with the sitter. You may want to explain how you are going to do this by saying you are going to draw a shape (usually a circle but it can be any shape and size), and in it you are going to draw a symbol, pattern or picture depending on the impressions you receive. Reassure the sitter that you will not be touching the person, only assessing their energy field which can be done through paranormally sensing.

2. After answering any questions which may come from the sitter, begin to draw the aura-graph shape you are going to use for this exercise , that is; the full figure of the person you have been inspired to do this for, and begin the drawing. You may, at first, only want to draw symbols or use the colour and images you receive, however as you practice this exercise you will gain more confidence and become better at drawing things you can only see in your mind's eye.

3. I have seen several aura-graphs in the history of the paranormal books and they are all different. Charles W Leadbeater, a Theosophist with Madame Blavatsky, drew and painted some of the first aura-graphs in his book *Man Visible and Invisible* which relates mostly to the physical, mental and emotional auras, and yet Nelson Ross, a Spiritualist, always created his sketches inside a circle which were predominately landscapes with drawings of birds and animals. The medium and healer, Stella Upton at the Arthur Findlay College, draws, and colours with pencils, small landscapes inside a circle which she then reads and interprets for the sitter.

4. Once you have the outline you will then need to 'tune into' the sitter's aura and start to draw and colour the picture. Try not to think too much about what you are doing just go with your first impressions. At first draw without talking about what is being drawn onto the paper, but let the impressions and images, which get better as you practice, speak for themselves, then you will be able to talk as you go along.

5. As you are drawing write down impressions, as with the other two exercises, and interpret the words, images, feelings at the end. The interpretation of the drawing is always at the end when you will need to ask your sitter if the reading made any sense to them.

Obviously with psychic readings much of the information which comes through to you will be at a physical level but as you go along and do more, you may find that information comes into the drawing which doesn't make any sense at the time, but it will when your sitter has time to think the reading over.

6. Finally, the more often you practice the exercises the better you will get. The most important aspect when working with psychic art is to raise an awareness within your sitters to the fact that their life force and psychic energy can be tangible to psychics and sensitive's, and that it can be drawn and painted. Yet for what reason? Why should we want to do this? Well I believe it is to help others understand that the invisible energies around them can be can be assessed and changed. If it is negativity that is causing problems, then that can be discharged by drawing the energy on the paper, if it is positive energy, it can be shared.

Psychic art is a means to an end. It is serious and yet can be very enjoyable to do. Remember to keep the journal and take photographs as you progress, then you will see how you have developed through the exercises. Use your imagination and use the exercises as starting points to your own creativity. Decide which of the exercises went well for you and which didn't. Practice and more practice will make you better at it and don't forget to share your good practice with other people. Once you have mastered the art of the psychic then it will be time to move on to the next stage of drawing and painting the spirit world in all its light and glory.

Spirit Art

Spirit art, unlike psychic art, is developed with the involvement of spirit. However, because the manifestation of spirit art is created by attaining different levels of awareness, some of the following exercises can be completed straight away but the later ones may need you to work on your own psychic development before they can be attained. This is a matter for you to decide and accept when you need to move from one exercise to the next.

If, when you are creating art for your private readings, you find your sitters are saying 'yes' to all you say and they can recognise the portraits or images you produce then go ahead through the exercises. If they are uncertain about your information or drawing or saying 'no' then more practice is needed. For those of you who are artists already then the drawing should be no problem, it may be the giving of the message which may need practice and if you are a medium already the opposite may be true. Above all the essence of spirit art is the evidence from the art work and the message it gives. Once the evidence is in place then move on to the next exercise because you know you are capable of drawing spirit art.

Unlike the preparation for psychic art there is more of a need to meditate and calm the outer body before creating spirit art in order to connect with your inner spirit, or spirit mind, which makes that tentative connection with the spirit world. From your meditations you may 'see' the person you want to draw and so you can work on the paintings straight away. It may be that when your sitter comes into your sacred space you begin to get a 'feel' for the spirit person and then you can start. On some occasions the spirit sense or vision does not happen straight away and you may be told clairaudiently from the spirit world that the person to be drawn is a lady and round-faced so you will start to draw from the verbal spirit description.

Information can come to you in a variety of ways; you may be given a verbal description, you may see the spirit person in your mind's eye or you may sense the build of the spirit. It is the latter which often amuses my students. How can you sense a red beard or hair? Well, it is not easy to explain but you can. It is all about using your paranormal senses and not your normal senses. Sensing a man with a moustache and elongated face will be relative to your own. I have a round face and no moustache so it is easier to me to sense the difference, my face may feel longer and I may be able to sense thick hair above my upper lip, just as I can sense the man is a lot taller than me. It's easier to understand once you have done it and most of the first spirit portraits drawn are created using this method.

Art is all about visual communication and even when a drawing is naïve or child-like a recipient can still recognise their loved one. At a church service in the 1980's I had put all my art equipment away ready to finish when I saw a gentleman in spirit. I took out a piece of paper and pencil and, in a matter of seconds I drew a sketch of an elderly man with a moustache. His forehead seemed too large for the rest of the face but his son still recognised him and was glad to receive the portrait. The next visit to the church the gentleman brought the portrait to me with a small black and white photograph of his father. The photo and drawing were identical and the son even said that his father had a very large forehead. So, if I had changed the drawing to fit my artistic sensibilities then it would have been wrong!

For those of you who think you can't draw you might find my DVD 'Developing Spirit Art' of some help or go to the Library or buy a book on drawing portraits. You only need to know the basics and that is all I teach, with some wondrous results, in my workshops. You never know what you can do until you try. In the first exercise I will describe to you how to draw the guide lines of a face to help and then you can just copy them over and over again while developing your spirit portraiture.

Below are three exercises, one, how to draw a portrait, two, details how to start drawing spirit portraits and three spirit guides. There is also one more section detailing how other spirit art work can be developed in pastel, pencil and paint. All exercises should be done in your area you call sacred space after you have calmed your physical mind.

Exercise One

Drawing a portrait

For this exercise you will need a pencil and a piece of A4 white paper. You are going to draw the template for a portrait showing the basic guidelines you will need to follow when starting your spirit portraiture.

1. Draw an oval on the paper large enough for the length of your hand to fit in with space above and below the hand and the oval.
2. Draw a line down the centre of the oval
3. Draw a line across the centre of the oval. Make sure this is in the centre, not too high or too low, these guidelines are very important to the balance of the face you are going to draw.
4. Ignoring the space above the centre horizontal line draw a line in the centre between the main horizontal line and the bottom of the oval

5. Draw another line below the in the centre below the one you have just drawn and the bottom of the oval.

6. So, you should now have an oval with a centre vertical line and three horizontal lines one below the other from the centre.

7. Come back to the centre horizontal line and mark four dots; two either side of the vertical line to indicate where the eyes are. These dots should be the same distance apart as the lengths of the each eye, so, draw a circle at the crossover of the vertical and horizontal line with two lemon shapes between the last set of dots, the circle should be in the middle of the lemons. These are the eyes

8. Come down to the centre crossover line below the eyes and draw a small 'u' shape stretching either side of the centre but only an inch long in total. Go down to the third line and draw a lines of about two inches, in total, along that line either side of the vertical line, this is the mouth.

9. The ears are like long 'm' shapes either side of the head level with the eyes and the bottom of the nose. The hairline comes down about 2-3 inches below the top of the oval and above the eyes.

And there you have your template for the face. Once you feel the proportions are right then go over all the lines with a black felt tip pen. A template is used over and over again as the basis for a portrait drawing and can be used underneath thinner paper so the guidelines, or grid, for the portrait does not have to be drawn over and over again. Keep it somewhere safe or you will have to draw another one.

Drawing a spirit portrait

You will need paper, (the size and type to suit you but A3 is good for portraits), pencils, pastels, putty eraser. You should place the paper with the longer side upright, (this is known as 'portrait' when the paper is shorter side upright the orientation of the paper is known as 'landscape'). The creative process of drawing spirit portraits should be conducted in a place of peace. You may see me rushing onto a stage or platform after being stuck in traffic jam to get to the venue, and then start to draw spirit portraits, but I have been doing this for a long time and am able to make a link with spirit just by sending out a thought to the spirit world.

When you first start drawing or committing yourself to doing anything concerning mediumship, try to bring that sacred space around you by meditating on the higher energies. As you do so you will begin to make a connection with higher forces, remembering what I suggested before about beginning to feel changes in your energy environment, seeing, sensing or hearing descriptions from another world. Once that begins to happen then it will be time to start the drawing. You do not have to have a sitter present because the spiritual energies know who the drawing is for but at first I think it would be best to either have a sitter or think about a person while you are doing the drawing.

Draw the person you sense and write down any names, places, objects which come to mind because later you will find that the impressions will mean something to the recipient. Never discount anything while you are working with the higher forces because even a white elephant may mean something to your sitter.

Exercise Two

Creating a spirit portrait

Have your template ready and if you feel you can't draw a portrait without it place the template under the paper you are about the draw on and copy the main features, the outline of the head, the ears, eyes, mouth and nose and use the marks as a guide to where the features of the face should be, remembering that all faces are different and the face should be a guide only You will need to change the features the way you feel the face should look. Ask your guide, your art teacher or artist in the spirit world to help you.

1. Tune into the higher forces and ask for help. It is important to ask because in the spirit world there will be someone who wants to help you do this and if you don't ask then they will not force themselves on you. One of my spirit art students, when asked to draw the person who was helping him, drew a very good portrait of a friend

of mine who was an art teacher, so my friend in spirit, who was an exceptional artist and teacher, was helping the student that time. You probably won't have Leonardo Da Vinci when you first start but you will have someone who was able to teach or lecture in art and those people in spirit, who really want to help, find someone who is like them. If they used colour you will be inspired to use colour. Work with them. Spirit art is a mutual creation between the earth and the spirit, and we cannot work without them.

2. Once you have begun to sense a portrait, begin the drawing using the art equipment you have around you. Try to start and finish the drawing in one go and write to the side of the drawing, or on another piece of paper, the names, places, visions you see, and the objects, animals which the spirit world bring to you.

3. Once the drawing is complete you can then show it to the recipient and begin to give the verbal evidence. If the drawing is not quite right or not recognised DO NOT WORRY. One of my drawing's, which was drawn during a spirit art demonstration at Wolverhampton Church, took 15 years to be recognised. When a family member visited from Australia with photographs of the family the portrait was recognised so sometimes the recipient actually does not know the spirit person and it is not you producing wrong spirit art.

4. Once you have shown the portrait to the sitter and you are giving the information to go with it you may find that the reading becomes clear. There is a system which you may want to use when you are giving the information which can help the sitter understand why this particular person has come to them and why.

5. A reading could be done this way; give information based on who the person was, for example; what relationship to the sitter were they, what did they do for a living, what did they died of or how did they pass? Did they have any individual personality traits or hobbies? Then find out the reason for the drawing. Ask questions of the spirit, such as; why have they come to speak to the sitter, did they have something in common and was attracted to the reading because of this experience, do they want to re-assure the sitter of something they had, (i.e. health problem) or did (work connection).

Give the sitter a chance to reply and remember that sometimes a young person may never have met their grandfather but could go away and find a photograph to see if the portrait is correct.

6. Once the reading is complete, and a typical reading should take around 30 to 45 minutes with a drawing, any longer and you are pulling on your psychic energies which will tire you out, give the portrait to the person and thank the spirit world for helping you. I always hear from my guides, 'And, thank you too!' when I finish my work. If I remember to do this, I usually take a photograph of the artwork to keep a record. Very few of my drawings look alike so people can't say I am drawing the same person all the time so try to make sure you are drawing faces from spirit and not what you think you should draw.

Drawing spirit art is unique and the process cannot be learnt in a day. The more you do the better the drawing gets and the closer you work with your guides, art teachers and artists. I seem to have a wide range of artists and helpers because, over the years, I have noticed different styles coming through when I work automatically.

Exercise Three

Developing your drawing style and advancing your mediumship

Once you have learnt how to make that link with the spirit world and you feel confident about the drawings you are doing, and you are receiving positive responses from your sitters it is time to try the next exercise. This exercise is to help you loosen up your drawing hand to allow more information to come through and to help you. This exercise is the first step to automatic drawing which will allow your artist guide to control your hand and draw the portrait for you. There is a type of mediumship called *automatic writing* whereby the medium will sit with a pen or pencil in his or her hand and allow their hand firstly to scribble and then to write.

Vale Owen, a Church of England Minister, who, with the aid of his deceased mother, wrote a book called 'Beyond the Veil', by using automatic writing. His mother controlled his hand and wrote stories about life in the spirit world. Taking this method a stage further I allow my spirit artist to control the part of my brain, which moves my hand, in order to draw some of my spirit portraits. The drawings are accepted by sitters or people in an audience during a demonstration so I allow this to happen.

Our exercise is not going to take you that far but you will need to move your consciousness away from your ordinary drawing method and allow your hand to move in its own way. At first your attempts may just be scribble but once you 'let go' you will find the exercise will help you. You will need your paper and pencils to hand. I would use a 6B graphic pencil for this and A3 paper to give you space in which to extend the drawing to wherever it wants to go. Try not to restrict your hand movements on the page and if the drawing is larger than the paper use bigger paper.

This is what you need to do;

1. Working in sacred space, and with enough paper in front of you, place the pencil lightly in your preferred hand

2. Ask your guides to come forward to help

3. Place the lightly grasped pencil onto the paper and breathe in and out three times to bring your spirit guide towards you to you.

4. Build up the energy around you by visualising your auric space getting brighter and more powerful each time you breathe.

5. You may start to feel the pencil move but if not start to move it slightly yourself to start the movement going. Close your eyes and let the energies move your hand.

6. Your first attempts may be scribble like the psychic scrying exercise but as you persevere you will find the marks become more readable.

7. Once you have started the pencil scribbling try this next simple exercise. Start the pencil moving so that you begin to draw an oval going over and over the oval many times getting faster and faster. Then allow the spirit to move your hand into the oval in an attempt to start to draw the features of the face. Don't let your sub-conscious get in the way at this point because you will find yourself, saying to yourself, 'is this me doing the drawing?'. I would like to say to you that if you have put out to the spirit world the intention

to create a spirit drawing, then that is what you will get. Try to think of anything else but the drawing and you will find that some sort of recognisable drawing will be created.

8. Practice the above over and over again until the spirit artist has full use of your hand. I usually get a twitch on my drawing hand to tell me the artist is ready. You may receive the same or something different but just keep trying which will cement the bond between you and your artist.

9. Work with a couple of coloured pencils in your hand and do the same. See what happens. Start experimenting with pastels, conte crayons and felt tips and sometimes use coloured paper. Remember you are the artist too, you are learning by doing and even if you don't do a reading from this exercise you will have a lot of very interesting artwork to scry and look through.

10. The next stage for this exercise is to ask a sitter to come and work with you for a reading. Ask your guide to draw the portrait as you gather the verbal evidence while the drawing is being created. Once you start to receive positive reactions to the drawings then you know you are getting it right. Until then PLAY!

There are other exercises you can do but I feel you have enough in this section of the book to keep you going for a few years. The main aspect to all mediumship is not to get so preoccupied and consumed by it you forget to eat, feed the cat or the children, or it takes over your life. Spirit art should be part and parcel of your life not all consuming. Practice art techniques as much as you like, in painting and drawing pictures of your own choice you will bring your spirit artist closer to you. I am helped all the time by my artist guides in spirit when I need help with my own artwork and creativity, but they do not do everything for me, if they did I would not be an artist or person in my own right and the spirit world knows that, so you need to be firm with yourself and the spirit world when allowing them so close to you.

I suggest an hour a day for the meditation and sitting with spirit 30-45 minutes at the most. I always say to my students that the spirit world has a home and work to go to as well! Spirit art becomes a way of life once you have mastered it but don't let it take over.

Keeping Your Journal

The reason why you should keep your journal because it could now reflect your learning process over the time you have spent creating your sacred space, the types of music you have tried and decided on, the readings, making new (and different) spirit artworks and generally being creative. You should also have a group of people who have received drawings, paintings, aura-graphs and other paranormally produced artworks, who are very pleased with the images as well as the verbal information you have given to them. In it make a note of all your feelings, impressions, the ways you have worked, techniques and skills you have learnt along the way and also the pitfalls and elations which have made your artwork the way it is.

In time, you will be able to read the pages and see how far you have come. The experiences you have had and may want to share to help someone else do the same, or, by then, there may be other techniques and methods which you may want to add. Of course all this can be written on a computer and each stage saved to disc or whatever is available in the future. It has been a spectacular journey for you and your pathway will lead you to places, people and things you may never have dreamt about. Art is all about moving forward and changing the goalposts. If we all just keep doing the same thing forever then what we do will become stale. Try different ways of working, of thinking and of making that wonderful link with the spirit world and our friends over there.

The question is, do you want to take the artwork a stage further and begin to show what you are capable of to the general public? My next move was to begin to teach what I knew and to help others do what I do. I was invited by the Spiritualist Churches and individuals interested in the paranormal to teach workshops and classes in the development of spirit and psychic art in their churches and organisations in the UK and abroad. I absolutely love teaching and imparting knowledge to others. I was a school teacher and adult lecturer for over 30 years and so I had the skills already in place to do it, and, after all, once I eventually retired there would be a need for others to teach psychic and spirit art also.

My most memorable spirit art class was at Wolverhampton Spiritualists Church, opposite Wolverhampton Football Club on Molyneux Road, where people from all over the West Midlands came to learn spirit art. They came in hail, rain and snow and they loved the sessions. One said that it was like going back to school without the homework. During the football match season we could hear the singing, howling and cheering from the football supporters who were so close to the church we always knew when a goal was scored! It was here that we built our sacred space for the group, had our invocation meditation and created our drawings with closing meditations to thank our 'invisible' friends. The artwork was tried and tested as we went along and the week that the healing group were also at the church we drew spirit portraits for them also.

Another very memorable teaching group was a group of amateur artists on the edge of Derbyshire who invited me to lecture for one day on 'How to bring the spirit out in portraits'. I did not divulge I was a medium because it was not appropriate for that group, but they thoroughly enjoyed the day and said that they had learnt a lot about drawing portraits never mind the spirit! More recently I was asked to teach portraiture to the U3A (University of the Third Age) which was very rewarding, and also to a group of carers and those grieving in the local cancer Hospice, again in my role as lecturer and not medium.

Lecturing spirit art in a Spiritualist environment is much easier than working with a group who know little about the subject because I have to spend a great deal of time discussing the philosophical argument relating to the concept of the after-life and so the two sides to my art teaching rarely come together. However, I was once in a very difficult position when in a watercolour class I was teaching I had both a Methodist minister and a lady who knew I was a medium. She had come to learn watercolours and my remit for the class was to do just that, but when she began to discuss my mediumship to the class I felt it had to be nipped in the bud, having always kept my beliefs out of my academic work. It was later when her daughter, who I had taught in school, arrived at the class with a large canvas painting of a baby being lifted to the sky (heaven) by angelic hands that I wondered why I had always been so pedantic about my knowledge. Cathy brought the painting to me because she had lost a baby full term, whom she had named Matthew, and she wanted to know if she had painted the spirit of the baby correctly. The painting brought tears to many a student's eye because it was so beautiful and having lost a baby myself I thought it was so poignant. The vicar came to her and said that he wished he could see angels like us and the painting lifted his heart and he was glad to see it. Cathy told us she was going to take the painting to the chapel in the hospital where it still is.

Spirit Landscapes

Spirit landscapes can be painted after they are seen either in real-time, like the energy fields above the hill at Uffingham, or in the visions of the afterlife experienced in meditations. After you have mastered the art of spirit portraiture and drawing the objects the spirit world have shown you with the spirit person, try drawing and painting the images seen in meditation or while sensing energy fields, like auras, in landscapes or seascapes. The only thing which may be holding you back is you. The spirit world is there to be drawn and painted. I asked a student of spirit art to go into meditation and then ask the spirit world if he could see the landscape in the spirit world and the student drew a wonderful impression in pastel of the place I see when I go into my meditations. The spirit world is made of light and love, and you can now draw and paint what they look like. Once you see them paint them.

Teaching And Exhibiting Spirit Art

As a natural progression from drawing and painting the spirit world and starting to teach what I knew about spirit art I decided to engage a young film maker to make two teaching DVD's, one based on the development of psychic art and another on spirit art. As I was growing older, less fit, and less inclined to travel long distances by car and even further by airplane, the idea of the two DVD's came about. They would enable me to teach when I couldn't get to the venue but my DVD can. Hundreds all over the globe have been purchased and I always encourage those who buy them to let me know how they are progressing and hope they will show them to the public one day.

There are several ways of displaying and showing the work you have created and these are; exhibitions in art galleries, public demonstrations in community halls, spiritualist churches and theatres, and by teaching the art yourself and training others to do the same. Public demonstrations are a good way for showing spirit art to a lot of people. Sometimes the Spiritualist Churches invite the mediumistic artists to demonstrate what they do as a 'special' in order to earn a little money for the ever increasing costs to keep the churches running. The medium will receive travelling expenses and perhaps a fee but the best thing about these demonstrations is that the people understand the process of mediumship.

Spirit art is sought-after by some people and, sometimes, when a drawing is completed during the demonstration, they say, "Oh, yes I know that person", when they actually don't know the person in the portrait, all they want is to take a portrait home with them. I have had two women fighting over a portrait and the evening had to be stopped because they eventually stood up and were calling each other names. If you feel confident enough to publically demonstrate spirit art then do so, but be aware of the pit-falls along the way, perhaps start by organising your own evening of spirit art and go from there, or sit in on a demonstration working together with another artist, all experience will help.

Demonstrating spirit art in a theatre has its own problems. If you have a full theatre and you are using a microphone you may have to draw and speak the message into the microphone at the same time, sometimes it's better if you have a medium working with you and you can concentrate on the drawing. It is sometimes very difficult to hear the recipient unless they also have a microphone. At Leeds Variety Theatre, when I was working with Billy Roberts and his friends, we had to contend with people sitting in theatre boxes way up high in the theatre. These people, when the medium was looking up, were on a level with the stage lights, so, as well as trying to put a message across we had the powerful lighting system in our eyes too which was quite difficult to manage.

Village Halls and Community Centres are good venues, they are cheaper to organise and, as long as they have a small stage or platform, most people can be heard and seen by the medium when a response to the message is needed. If someone else is organising the event and venue make sure they know your requirements. For example, I am small and I don't wear high heels so if the event is organised where I am demonstrating on the same level as the audience then many will not be able to see me or the drawing being created which is a vital part of the evening. Try to politely suggest what you need and, if it is a charity event, ask for the bar to be closed while you are demonstrating. I have experienced several occasions when the organiser has thought it a good idea to improve the income on the evening to have the bar open while I have been demonstrating. When this happens not only do you have to put up with people moving in and out of their seats but also, as the evening wears on ,the audience can become progressively more intoxicated, noisy and sometimes argumentative. May I suggest the bar open before the demonstration and after so those who need a stiff drink can have one and when the evening has finished, just an hour and a half later, the bar is open again to satisfy their needs.

So, you can see that demonstrations for the general public can be quite difficult to handle. Set your limits and make sure you let those organising the evening know what you need. There have been times when I have travelled for many hours to a venue and only 6 people turned up, with; no cup of welcoming tea or food, Bingo being played in the adjoining room, and a four hour journey home. Many a time a bottle of water and a MacDonald's is what I have to keep me going! The demonstrations do help give you a sense of reality though. It is not all doom and gloom.

The Spirit Art Society

Exhibiting Your Art

Once you have collected a few of your evidential drawings together sittings, why not contact an Art Gallery and ask if you can exhibit? In my home town I have had five spirit art exhibitions, three group exhibitions with my students and two of my own work. The gallery is a council run gallery and I pay a small amount for the use of it. For the last three years the Spirit Art Society has an art exhibition so that those who wish to exhibit their artwork have a platform to do so. Artists from Europe, USA and Ireland have exhibited their spirit art in the past and they have shown that artwork can be created by any country, language, culture and religion.

One of the spirit art exhibitions has been of the portraits I have painted on canvas of the spirit people I have seen in the town. One of these paintings was the *Lady in Grey*, who used to haunt the Ancient High House, which is a fifteenth century building in the centre of Stafford. The Lady was never seen again once her portrait was painted. Another spirit portrait was of the Victorian housekeeper who lived in Walton Hall, now a restaurant and hotel with conference facility. I saw her on my fiftieth birthday when I had lunch there with a couple of friends. My friend heard the jingle of her keys and another felt the chill of her presence. I saw her and went home to paint her portrait, that of a rotund woman with a bunch of keys around her waist which were good enough for a jailer.

It has been said that one winter's night, not so long after, when the waiters and kitchen staff were on their way home after a long night, they decided to leave the tidying up of the tables until they came in the following day. This they did and when they returned the following day all the tables were cleared and neatly set. No-one owned up to doing it and the blame was placed squarely onto the spirit housekeeper. This particular painting, was painted in acrylic paint on canvas and has been given to the restaurant, however, unlike the Lady in Grey, the Housekeeper still keeps a watchful eye over her house.

Another canvas painting, which was exhibited in my second exhibition, was that of 'The Melting Pyramid', which was inspired after a visit from Lady Diana Spencer after her passing to the spirit world. In my vision of her I saw her as a series of parts which was very unlike other images I have painted. Firstly, her startling and unusual eyes appeared to me, followed by her expressive smile and face and then her hair. I could hear her voice clairaudiently, but I was watching the images form in front of me which I painted. There was a full moon that appeared at her forehead and a melting pyramid (which was very like the Salvador Dali impression of the melting watch) below her eyes with a river in-between. The impression lasted for about a minute and shortly after when I had come out of the meditation I started to paint the canvas. When I exhibited the symbolically styled painting there was only one person who recognised who I had painted and she said she knew straight away because of the distinctive eyes, and she also understood the meaning behind the symbols. I was happy I had done a good job in hiding the message behind the portrait, for not all messages are meant to be publicly announced.

The three public group exhibitions of spirit art came about after I founded the Spirit Art Society in 2008. The Society was set up to encourage spirit artists to exhibit in the gallery or on line. I built a simple web site to let everyone know it was there with an explanation of what spirit art was and why we, as a group, wanted to let people know it existed. In the first exhibition we had three spirit art students and a lady from Sweden exhibit, and the in second exhibition there were seven students, a lady from Sweden and an artist from Virginia in USA. The second show also had spirit photography from two exhibitors and the stories of how they appeared alongside them. I hope this is an indication that with time the exhibitions will grow with more people exhibiting, from more countries and with more spirit photography. For some people who visited and left comments in the comments book, they said they had never seen anything like it and because much of the work was evidential in nature, the exhibition was thoroughly 'thought provoking'. The Spirit Art Society has given spirit art an opening into the greater scheme of world-wide information and has attracted many people interested in the artworks from around the globe. The exhibitions are showing that more people are interested in both exhibiting and learning the techniques.

The Spirit Art Society was formed because the hundreds of art works produced by several psychic and spirit artists at demonstrations, workshops and in private readings were inadvertently being lost in the back of cupboards in people's homes. While I was researching spirit art for my Master of Philosophy thesis I realised that much of the artwork created by our past artists, Coral Polge, Ivor James and Frank Leah, together with the working artists of today were given away without records being taken of them. No one knows where the drawings are from our past masters because the artworks were never recorded. Who were the drawings of, which materials were used, where were the drawings created and why? The answers to these questions are lost through the passage of time.

For over a year I was looking for information regarding the pre-war spirit artist Frank Leah. I found a quote about him in the book *This is Spiritualism* by Maurice Barbanell (1959) p 135:

> 'Frank Leah is an artist for whom the dead pose in his studio. For thirty years he has used his combined talents of clairvoyance and artistry to portray thousands of dead women and children.'

While chatting to Margaret Davis, another medium, at a funeral, I was told that there was a small book written about him which was very rare. Leah's work, almost lost to history, was captured in a small book, *Faces of the Living Dead*, by Paul Millar in 1943, finding this book gave me great encouragement to carry on creating spirit art. This book has now been reprinted, (2010), so if you are interested you could find in on the Internet.

In 1985, while visiting Daulby Street Spiritualist Church in Liverpool, I watched Coral Polge give a demonstration of spirit art and received a message. Coral was selling her book, *Living Images*, (1991), after the demonstration and I went to her to buy the copy I still have. While I waited she turned to me and said that when she retired there will be a need for someone who was artistic to carry spirit art on. With her help in spirit I have been able to do just that and, hopefully, bring spirit art and artists together to help each other. It must have been such a strain on her since there were very few artist mediums at that time. Ivor James, another prolific spirit artist in the 1970's to 1980's was influenced by Coral Polge, as was Alan Stuttle watercolourist and psychic artist.

I met Ivor James at Daulby Street Spiritualist Church in Liverpool while he was demonstrating an evening of spirit art, and something happened to him that has sometimes occurred when I have been demonstrating, and that was, what we call a split link. Mr James was drawing a portrait while giving some verbal evidence and myself and another lady could accept all the information including the name Bridge. So, Mr James asked for something from spirit which would split the link in order to ascertain who the drawing was for. He said, "Mother Shipton's Well", and as he did so turned the drawing around for us to see and it was a wonderful drawing of my auntie who lived next to Mother Shipton's Well in Knaresborough, Yorkshire. The other lady could not take that evidence and the drawing came to me. It is those in spirit who can decide who the drawing is for when there is a split link, and I always feel uplifted when the drawing goes to the right person.

The Spirit Art Society offers an opportunity to psychic and spirit artists to exhibit their hard-copy art work in a yearly exhibition, or, over the ether on the internet web site, or attend regular meetings or workshops. Spirit artists can often feel isolated because of their fine tuned art work and the Society gives them an opportunity to get together and advance their techniques both in artistry and in the mechanics of mediumship. While the teaching of mediumship is booming, spirit art could quite possibly be left behind, unless we do exhibit and show the general public what we create with the help of spirit.

Chapter Eleven

WHAT COMES NEXT?

In previous chapters I have written about myself, how I realised I was mediumistic, how I was able to combine mediumship with art and how I have encouraged others by teaching them what I know about psychic and spirit art. For the potential spirit art student I have detailed the process and techniques involved in the production of the art together with methods of how to create your own specialist art and how to give psychic and spiritual readings with the art you produce. I have written about the risks and responsibilities which is part and parcel of any form of paranormal activity and when you work how to build your own form of sacred space.

You now have all the ingredients for building up your psychic and spiritual art portfolio, but what are you going to do with all the hard work and energy you have invested in doing all this? What can you do with the work you have created other than giving them away to your sitters? That is entirely up to you. Hopefully, you will encourage others to do the same, develop new and better skills than the ones I have given you, demonstrate and exhibit your work to the general public.

The message is simple. Mediumship, in the form of spirit art, is produced in order to help people understand the spirit world and the concept of the afterlife. A spiritualist is someone who believes in the spirit world because they have received their evidential proof of the spirit surviving mortal death. A portrait is additional evidence for them. Having a portrait given to you by someone who is a stranger and who has never met your loved one, or friend is remarkable in the least, but to also give their name, address and how they died is mind blowing.

As a spiritualist, who was influenced while a child by the Roman Catholic faith, and as an adult, Tibetan Buddhism, I have an accumulation of beliefs. But, these beliefs did not make me a medium that is able to see the invisible world which coincides and co-exists with the physical world, because that particular faculty came with me when I was born. Being able to draw competently is an ability which people seem to be born with. Some people call these abilities 'gifts'. It is my understanding that being able to see into another world is also a faculty which some people are born with, and that not all, who have it, use it in the same way as others. Like artists and musicians some people are born with these abilities but never use them. It may not be their pathway in this life for them.

Being a medium has nothing to do with age, gender, religion or belief; ethnic, social, economic grouping or any other constrict of birth or breeding, it is to do with our fundamental genetic make-up and the spiritual choices we have made before birth. The former statement is quite easy to understand since science is coming up with more and more information regarding our genes and physical make-up. In fact I was in my 50's before I knew that I was born with a life changing genetic mutation which needs regular hospital treatment to avoid terminal illness. It seems that because my ancestors did not have regular food, their gene mutated so that iron would be kept in the body to stop the clan from dying out. Obviously, when food is in plenty, we no longer need the extra iron, so today, the mutation is life threatening.

There are some lines of thought which say that we decide our outcome before we are born and that we also plan our destiny, the people we need to meet, the places we need to go to and what we need to do with our life in order to make sure that destiny unfolds itself. It is also thought that we are able, during life to make changes to that plan, through what is known as 'free will'. Mediumship is not really about fortune telling and asking a third party, someone we don't know, to plan our life, it is about what we can learn while we are on the physical earth. It is about how we can help others. It is said that Buddha would not go through the gates of heaven until all mankind is there before him. It is about learning, experiencing and following a spiritual way of life. What I have just said does not mean being religious, although if we want to we can, it means that we have a humanitarian approach to life and that all people on the earth have a spirit which survives mortal death. We are all born naked, most of us have our vital organs in approximately the same place in order to live and when we return to spirit we are known by our spiritual light. That is, our light is the spiritual progress we have made in our life on the earth, and that light is made up of love. And the love is made up of the way we are with people and animals living around us, including the people who test us the most, giving us the light we hold.

Choosing a path of mediumship is not the easiest of journeys to take. The first thing we do when we realise we have this supernatural faculty is open ourselves up to every-other-mans' thoughts, feelings and sensations, and, we are then asked by others to talk to their deceased family members who are sometimes in the room with you hours before their relation arrives. On one occasion I was asked by a woman to speak to her new boyfriend's deceased wife, to find out if the widower, and his wife's, sex life was as he said it was. This is not what I signed up to do! Sometimes when eating out or around and about in my local town my spirit reception, like the tuning on a radio, I can get stuck and I am open to all the spirit people around me. I have had a lot of training and practice and I know it is best not to be in that open state, so I mindfully close my inner self down to the spirit world when leading my earthly life.

Mediumship, in many ways can be a curse as well as a wondrous ability. The down side, and I feel you should be aware of this if you are thinking of taking the journey, is that you will lose old friends because they do not want to hear your news about the dead people you talk to, some family members will no longer be phoning you and you will be taken off their Christmas card list. People will come out of nowhere wanting to know their future, even if you tell them you only draw portraits and work with spirit and don't do future events, and you will be asked to come to lunch or dinner only to be left alone at the end with one of the family who really needs to know something about their work or philandering husband. There's no such thing as a free lunch. On the brighter side, it is when you have that lovely link with spirit and the light shines all around you as you bring forward the child who passed suddenly with an illness which had not been recognised by the doctor, and the mum or dad who can sense the closeness of the spirit with them, as your energy brings their light and love through to be drawn for the parents. That's what it is all about!

Looking to the future, while psychics and mediums are talking about their communications from the spirit world and messages of past, present and future events to the general public, spirit art seems to be locked into a time warp from the nineteenth century still developing messages alongside an evidential portrait. Perhaps what we need now is more mediums describing to the artists what they can see, sense and feel when they journey into the spirit world so the artist can draw and paint the impressions. On the other hand, as an artist and a medium I paint all that I see when journeying into the other world so, perhaps, other artist-mediums may want to do the same.

My art work now is just that, paintings of spirit-scapes. I have proved I am a medium by producing hundreds of portraits of people in the spirit world so I have a certain credibility in psychic circles as to the authenticity of the pictures I draw, and, unlike visionary, outsider or eidetic art, the impressions I receive are implicitly from outside my range of experience and knowledge, coming direct from the world of spirit and its many levels.

Once, while painting a spirit landscape, I began to feel as though I was detached from my physical body and began walking (floating) into the picture. As my hand was painting I was inside the picture frame walking with spirit children who took me to a small amphitheatre. The open theatre-in-the-round was full of brightly lit young and old spirit people who were waiting for something, or someone, to start. I sat on one of the higher seats and waited until a light shone down from the sky into the centre of the theatre from which a seemingly elderly man appeared and began to speak. The audience had been waiting for one of the Elders to give his philosophical talk to those present. What a beautiful and inspirational experience!

Images, sounds and sensations of pure love filled the air, my head, my heart, and those all around me. Those profound impressions from the world of spirit will never be forgotten.
*

Perhaps this experience will be my next painting!
***